tacolicious

tacolicious

FESTIVE RECIPES FOR
TACOS, SNACKS, COCKTAILS, AND MORE

SARA DESERAN
with
JOE HARGRAVE, ANTELMO FARIA, AND MIKE BARROW

PHOTOGRAPHY BY ALEX FARNUM

TEN SPEED PRESS
Berkeley

To Mia, Moss, and Silas, who came about
long before their namesake drinks

Contents

Cocktails, Aguas Frescas + More **157**

Syrups, salts, and infusions

Infused tequilas

Cocktails

Agua frescas and other G-rated drinks

Gracias

From Sara

Recipe testers are like life insurance for a cookbook, and we had a few awesome ones, including Ann Deseran (or Nana, as she's known around here) and her sidekick, Andy (aka Grandpa), who made more than a few new friends as they threw countless Mexican feasts at their house in Sonoma.

Then there's the supremely stylish Lauren Godfrey, the food blogger of wegolden.com and owner of the gorgeous San Francisco home where we shot much of the photography. Lauren even woke up early one morning to get a tamale-making lesson from our cook Virginia Hinojosa (and then made the laborious tamales twice more just to be sure she got the recipe right).

Despite their hectic jobs, Mike Barrow, our director of beverage, and Telmo Faria, our executive chef, set aside their time to work on this book. This is not to mention T-lish chefs Mike Garcia and Caitlin Olmstead, and their kitchen staff, who found time to help develop and test recipes, as did our bar managers, Jeremy Harris and Josh Forth.

We love photographer Alex Farnum because he's the best (and not because he's a regular at Tacolicious), and we feel similarly about creative director Emma Campion (who, back in our nascent days, hired Tacolicious to cater her wedding). Thanks to Emily Timberlake, Jenny Wapner, and copy editor Sharon Silva for making us seem smarter, and to stylist Christine Wolheim for outfitting the food in such cool attire and sporadically breaking into dance throughout the shoot.

And of course I owe tons of thanks to Joe, the deep-diver in this relationship. Tacolicious wouldn't be the same without his drive, his creativity, his recado, and his love of vintage juice squeezers.

From Joe

Thanks to my mom, for caring about design, and to my dad, for being such great leader. You gave me a childhood full of Mexico, chores, and good food. It's almost as if you had a plan.

To Jack S. and Mike H. and Jason P. and Saul P., for meeting me at Circa that sad winter night in 2009 and for not laughing at the idea of our little Spanish restaurant becoming something called Tacolicious.

To Mia and Silas and Moss, for being such good eaters and choosing to "save" tacos over just about anything (except dumplings, which is a tie). To Lulu and Dexter and the good people at CUESA, for letting us be part of the fantastic Thursday market. And to Lisa at Williams-Sonoma for being such a great cheerleader.

Most of all, to my taco family: Sara, Mikey, Erin, Kory, Telmo—the list goes on—along with our investors, customers, and wonderful staff. Tacolicious is only as good as the sum of her parts. And from my perspective, she's pretty darn great.

Introduction

It was January 2009, on a seemingly normal Thursday night at Laïola, the Spanish restaurant that my husband, Joe, owned in the Marina District of San Francisco. The Tempranillo was being poured, the croquettes were piping hot. And then Rick Bayless walked in.

Coincidentally—or perhaps fatefully—Joe and I were headed to Mexico the next day for some much-needed R & R. The economy was in a tailspin. Restaurants were closing at an alarming rate in San Francisco, and the recession's maelstrom was sucking Laïola in, too—no matter that it had opened to three stars. Joe's stress level was at an all-time high. Our plan was to fly into Mexico City for a few nights, then spend the rest of our vacation on the beaches of the Yucatán, drinking a lot of tequila and burying our heads in the sand. Our hope was that when we returned to San Francisco the storm would have passed.

> Every time we return to Mexico, we are reminded not only of how delicious and vibrant the food is but also of how kind and warm the people are. Mexico is a country that embraces you.

So at Laïola that night, Joe nervously approached the Chicago-based restaurateur and the country's honorary professor of Mexican cuisine to ask where we should eat when we were in Mexico City, or DF (Distrito Federal), as the locals call it. Although we had both traveled to other parts of Mexico, from Veracruz to Guanajuato, we had used DF only as an airport transfer point. Amazingly, Mr. Bayless took the time to grab a pencil and a piece of paper and write out a long list of recommendations, as if the request weren't something he was asked every day.

Joe came home giddily waving around the paper as if we'd won the lottery. In a way, we had. That list kick-started an already brewing love affair with the food of Mexico, and most important, it was the beginning of Tacolicious.

o   o   o

Today, five years into Tacolicious, Joe and I have traveled to Mexico more times than we can count. We've driven the back roads of the Yucatán to bucolic, off-the-grid villages, such as Tekit, to visit the families of some of our cooks. We've mindlessly lounged on the beaches of Nayarit. We've gone on tequila tastings, traveling throughout the lowlands and the highlands of the tequila region, just outside of the stately city of Guadalajara. Every time we return to Mexico, we

When I met Joe, he carried a small plastic bag filled with a chipotle chile–based recado around in the glove box of his car (see page 38), right on top of the insurance papers. Because you just never know when you're going to need to spice things up.

are reminded not only of how delicious and vibrant the food is but also of how kind and warm the people are. Mexico is a country that embraces you.

While Joe and I might love Mexican food equally, our relationship with it blossomed in very different ways. Joe had the advantage of growing up in Modesto, California, in the heart of the Central Valley, a farm town with a large Mexican population. The Crow's Landing neighborhood is home to more taco trucks than I've ever seen in one place. To top it off, Joe was plucked out of school for months at a time by his parents, packed into a VW van with his brother and sisters, and driven, catamaran in tow, down to Baja to camp on the beach. He still wistfully recalls eating freshly made tortillas sold from the back of a pickup during those seaside sojourns.

Meanwhile, I was raised in Baton Rouge, Louisiana, where gumbo is for dinner (enchiladas, not so much). This doesn't mean that my mom didn't make us tacos, however. They were the deliciously bastardized version that Americans love so: Ortega hard shells filled with ground beef, tomatoes, lettuce, and cheddar cheese. You know the ones. Later on, while attending the University of California at Santa Cruz, where taquerias abound, I lived on burritos, the ultimate student fare and a gateway drug to more traditional Mexican cuisine.

I graduated from college and moved to San Francisco, working my way up as a food writer and an editor. Though Joe and I didn't know each other then, he was working in restaurants, starting in the early 1990s, as the general manager for Restaurant LuLu, helmed by Reed Hearon, at the time one of the city's most celebrated chefs. Incidentally, Hearon also operated Cafe Marimba, a regionally savvy Mexican restaurant that was ahead of its time. In those days, the San Francisco dining scene was identified with what was called Mediterranean food. Yet, if restaurant-goers were honest, Mexican food was much more integral to the local landscape. It just wasn't considered as sophisticated. In San Francisco, with few exceptions, Mexican food was almost solely found in the mom-and-pop taquerias and no-frills dinner houses that ruled the city's Mission District.

Fast-forward to 2007, and while Joe had opened a Spanish restaurant (and we had met and fallen in love because I loved the food there), at home, he still spent his personal time cooking Mexican food simply because he loved to eat it. I'm not kidding when I say that when I met Joe, he carried a small plastic bag filled with a chipotle chile–based *recado* around in the glove box of his car (see page 38), right on top of the insurance papers. Because you just never know when you're going to need to spice things up.

○ ○ ○

So Joe and I were in Mexico City, Rick Bayless's notes stashed carefully in Joe's wallet. We had booked a room at a wonderful bed-and-breakfast called The Red Tree House, located in Condesa, one of the city's chicest neighborhoods. Mellow, tree-lined streets, a mix of art deco and art nouveau architecture, chirping birds—all relatively cloistered from what can be a sprawling and traffic-ridden city. Wandering around, you'll see boutiques, nice restaurants, and *mezcalerias*. Roma, another lovely neighborhood, is a short walk away.

Per usual—museums and cathedrals and other historical sites be damned—the only true agenda Joe and I had was to eat well. And thanks to the excellent advice of Rick Bayless and others, what we experienced proved to be a game changer.

Aha! moment no. 1: Our first meal was just a few blocks from our B and B, at a restaurant called El Califa that was highly recommended by Jorge, our kind host. On a warm day, Joe and I sat down at one of the sidewalk tables and were served simple, thinly cut steak tacos. Unadorned, they were meant to be dressed up with a selection of the most exquisite salsas: a fresh serrano with chopped onion, a smoky and smooth chipotle, a chunky roasted tomato and jalapeño, and a dark and handsome guajillo. The ambience at El Califa is casual, but it isn't just a taqueria; it's a fusion between a taqueria and a full-service restaurant. And it has style. Our first reaction was, why isn't there something like this in San Francisco?

Aha! moment no. 2: This sentiment arose again when we headed over to one of Rick Bayless's top recommendations, Contramar, a lunch-only seafood brasserie-style restaurant in Roma staffed with waiters in crisp, ankle-length white aprons and black vests. The restaurant is full of see-and-be-seen professionals in suits enjoying some of the best food—Mexican or no—that Joe and I have eaten to this day. We shared a lunch of panfried soft-shell crabs that had been chopped and were served with a side of warm flour tortillas; we tried the kitchen's signature *pescado a la talla* (a beautiful fish that's butterflied and grilled, with one half topped with a red chile–based rub and the other with a parsley-based rub) accompanied with a dangerous little dish of marinated onions and habanero chiles; and we had the pièce de résistance, a tuna tostada made with raw ahi marinated

Per usual—museums and cathedrals and other historical sites be damned—the only true agenda Joe and I had was to eat well. And thanks to the excellent advice of Rick Bayless and others, what we experienced proved to be a game changer.

briefly in soy sauce and lime, dressed with a smear of just-spicy-enough chipotle mayonnaise, and topped with slices of fatty avocado and crispy fried leeks. An homage to this genius fusion dish is now a best-seller on our Tacolicious menu.

But it wasn't any specific dish that made our trip to Mexico City revelatory. It was a shift in our own perspective. Before we went on that trip, we tended to romanticize Mexican food as something that was at its best only if it was an *antojito* purchased from a street vendor or if it was prepared by a gorgeously wrinkled *abuela* in an embroidered dress—the stuff of *Saveur* magazine. Of course, these elements are part of the culture of Mexican cuisine. But suddenly we were experiencing Mexican restaurants in Mexico that were as hip and urban as restaurants in any sophisticated city and were completely void of the clichés Americans love to import: mariachi bands, heavy wooden furniture, servers dressed in *guayaberas*. San Francisco needed a taste of it. Selfishly, we wanted it for ourselves.

Back home, we kicked around ideas for bringing the food we'd found in DF to the States. One day, we got a call from Lulu Meyer, who was putting together a new Thursday farmers' market at the city's Ferry Building. Before we'd left for Mexico, she had asked us if we would do a Spanish food stand there and now wanted to know whether we'd decided on what we were going to sell.

Joe emailed her back with a crazy idea: "How about we sell tacos?"

Although Joe and I joked about naming our little Ferry Plaza farmers' market taco stand Fabuloso (a nod to Mexico's preferred and decidedly pungent all-purpose cleaner that's so ubiquitous that one whiff of it recalls our Mexico travels), we settled on Tacolicious, an equally frivolous name. It was just going to be a market stand, after all. Joe came up with a couple of *guisado* (braised meat) taco recipes—our now signature shot-and-a-beer chicken and our guajillo-braised short rib—put some grilled corn rubbed with his now-famous *recado* on the menu, and we were in business. On Thursdays, Joe would pack his SUV to the brim with food, haul it over to the waterfront market, and serve it up himself. Tacolicious was an instant hit. We had lines on day one. While Laïola continued to be dampened by the recession, Tacolicious, with its reasonable prices and cheerful comfort food, prospered. The writing was on the wall. And I believe it said "change or die."

Joe, Telmo, and Mike with our Paul Madonna mural as backdrop.

Whether it's the confluence of the warmth of chiles, the earthy aroma of tortillas, and the cheery zip of the salsas or just the humble ease of the cuisine itself, Mexican cooking, done well, is something that crosses borders.

So, on New Year's Eve 2009, we wistfully said goodbye to Laïola, taped up the windows, and, with the help of our parents and staff, painted the space, built a new bar (thanks to Joe's dad's woodworking skills), and hung artwork we'd commissioned from Paul Madonna on the walls. Only two weeks later—and after a near divorce over selecting a shade of teal for the room—we reopened as our first brick-and-mortar Tacolicious on Chestnut Street.

Three years later, there are now four busy Tacolicious restaurants—three in San Francisco and one in Palo Alto—all painted a spot-on teal (Joe was right) and serving our unabashedly Californian take on Mexican food. Tacolicious is a place where a chopped kale salad with quinoa shares menu space with a very traditional rendition of a *carnitas* taco. We have margaritas, of course, but we also have a drink called El Sangre, made with mezcal and blood orange and a hint of cinnamon. At Mosto, a tequila bar we opened next door to our Mission District location, we sell classic *tacos al pastor* straight from the spit alongside a bacon-wrapped hot dog with housemade relish. Our staff is made up of a happy mix of people from Mexico and people who simply love Mexico.

We have an amazing team of great folks, including Antelmo (Telmo) Faria, our fantastic executive chef, and Mike Barrow, our beverage director and the man behind our bar program (a rather staid title for someone who should really be called the T-lish Ninja). Together, these three amigos, Joe, Mike, and Telmo, have made countless trips to Mexico City, the tequila region, the Yucatán (where at least half of our kitchen staff is from), and beyond, bringing back scores of ideas for new dishes, new cocktails, and new tequilas. As for myself, when I'm not working as an editor, my role has been the chronicler of all things Tacolicious, which has included our website's blog (tacolicious.com), and now this cookbook.

Some days Joe and I just look at each other, both still in shock with the restaurants and their success. As much as we'd like to take the credit, we think there's something bigger going on here: Whether it's the confluence of the warmth of chiles, the earthy aroma of tortillas, and the cheery zip of the salsas or just the humble ease of the cuisine itself, Mexican cooking, done well, is something that crosses borders. People get hooked on it—all sorts of people. And once you find that you can easily cook it at home, you'll be a lifer. Trust us on this. We speak from experience.

How to cook from this book

Our restaurant, Tacolicious, serves a healthy mix of everything from chicken and rice soup to beet salad with housemade *queso fresco* to churros with chocolate sauce. However, this cookbook is focused on the core of our menu: tacos, tostadas, snacks, and all sorts of goodies that go great with a cocktail or an agua fresca. Start making an invite list now, because after mastering a few recipes, I promise that you're going to want to host a party.

Like any cuisine, Mexican cooking involves a lot of repetition, both in methods and in ingredients. The following techniques are basic but essential. Once you've got them down, you'll find that Mexican cooking is very forgiving, even user-friendly.

Toasting whole spices

Toasting almost any spice is a great way to bring out its flavor. To toast whole spices, put them in a small, dry, heavy skillet over medium heat. Stir for about a minute, until the aroma of the spice hits your nose. Transfer the spices to a clean spice grinder, let cool, then grind. (Store in a glass jar in a cool, dark cupboard for up to a month.) If you are using store-bought preground spices instead of whole spices that you toast and grind yourself, bump up the ground amount in the recipe slightly.

Briefly toasting dried Mexican oregano (yes, we know, this is an herb) the same way will yield similar results. No need to grind it; instead, just crumble it between your fingers as you add it to the dish.

Toasting, frying, and soaking dried chiles

Dried chiles are typically prepped a few different ways. To intensify their flavor, they are most often lightly toasted in a dry, heavy skillet for a minute or two, turning or stirring them to make sure they don't burn. Another technique is to fry them quickly in oil, which can actually make them spicier. (Some recipes don't call for toasting or frying the dried chiles at all.) Whatever you do, don't let the chiles burn, or turn black, which can ruin your whole dish. Erring on the side of undertoasted or underfried is much better!

Although some recipes call for grinding the toasted or fried chiles into a powder at this point, most require that you soak them in room-temperature water until softened before blending them into a sauce.

It is up to you whether or not you remove and discard the seeds of the chiles. Doing so eliminates a bit of heat, but it's also more work. Once they are stemmed, we usually throw the whole chiles in, seeds and all.

Roasting, broiling, and grilling vegetables

Many Mexican recipes call for roasting, broiling, or grilling vegetables and aromatics, commonly a rotating mix of onions, garlic, fresh chiles, tomatoes, or tomatillos. Part of the rationale is to cook the vegetables, but this step also imparts a smoky flavor. Oil is rarely used.

For consistency in this book, we chose broiling as the preferred method, but you can certainly experiment with roasting or grilling if you feel so inclined.

salsas,
pickles
+ more

21

You shouldn't judge a book by its cover, but we think you should judge a cook by his or her salsa. If anything speaks to the spirit and soul of Mexican food, it's this ubiquitous but never mundane table condiment.

A thoughtless salsa preparation is a sure sign that the rest of your meal isn't going to be all that hot (pun intended). Unfortunately, that's what you commonly get at many Mexican-American restaurants: a sloppy *salsa mexicana* (aka *pico de gallo, salsa fresca,* or *salsa huevona*) made with mushy, out-of-season raw tomatoes. But take solace in the fact that there is life beyond this uninspired preparation. If you've been repeatedly subjected to this default, you deserve a salsa awakening.

To dip into all of the varying types of salsas in Mexico is to begin to understand the breadth of Mexican cuisine. Although chiles, both dried and fresh, are invariably involved, a good salsa provides far more than a layer of heat.

There are glossy, smoky, almost raisiny, salsas made with dried chiles; spunky, fresh (*cruda*) salsas made with herbaceous raw chiles and tomatillos or other ingredients; and creamy, hauntingly spicy salsas made with peanuts and avocado. And although it is up to your personal taste, you'll find that every type of salsa has its definitive pairing, whether it's scrambled eggs, a roasted chicken, or a steak taco.

Some of the recipes in this chapter were inspired by salsa revelations we've experienced, specifically at El Califa in Mexico City. Although the tacos there are good, they are mostly a backdrop for the array of gorgeous salsas that accompany them. Thus, today at Tacolicious, every taco order is automatically served with a colorful trio of our now signature salsas.

But be forewarned: salsa stirrings often lead to obsessive behavior. I became fixated on a salsa that I'd had years ago in Bucerías, a beach town outside of Puerto Vallarta. Made of not much more than a smear of smoky charred chiles, some oil, and a squeeze of lime, it was a near-perfect pairing for fried-fish tacos. Telmo became infatuated with what he always knew as "orange sauce," a salsa from one of his favorite local taquerias in San Jose, California. Today, we serve his riff at Mosto, our tequila bar, usually with *tacos al pastor*, and you can make it at home by turning to page 35.

Two things will probably surprise many Americans. First, in Mexico, most salsas are not steam-out-of-your-ears-spicy (that is, unless you're in the habanero-loving Yucatán, where fire extinguishers should be served with dinner). Second, salsa is normally served as an accompaniment to food, not as a dip for tortilla chips. In a story on salsas in the *New York Times*, Javier Olmedo, a university student and would-be chef in Oaxaca, put it like this: "Watching someone shovel in salsa with tortilla chips is strange to Mexicans. Like how an American would feel watching someone drink salad dressing out of the bottle."

But who's to say that chips and salsa aren't a great pairing, even if the marriage was born in the United States? At Tacolicious, a meal doesn't start until our tomato-mint salsa and a bowl of freshly fried chips are placed on the table. Sometimes the bastardizations of a cuisine are among the tastiest.

Roasted tomato–mint salsa

Served with chips, this is the salsa that greets you when you sit down at Tacolicious. We make others, of course, but this is the one that seems to hit home with everyone. Although the ingredients are mostly expected, the uplifting note of fresh mint keeps diners guessing. The recipe was inspired by a chef whom Joe came of age with—Reed Hearon, one of San Francisco's former greats who cooked at Restaurant LuLu and Cafe Marimba. In our house, Hearon's cookbook, *La Parrilla*, is well worn and loved. Don't just limit this salsa to chips. It also pairs wonderfully with Three-chile bistec adobado (page 110), Carnitas (page 124), and Achiote-rubbed grilled chicken (page 134).

MAKES ABOUT 2¹/₂ CUPS

6 small Roma tomatoes, halved lengthwise

¹/₂ large yellow onion, sliced into ¹/₂-inch-thick rounds

1 small jalapeño chile, stemmed

¹/₄ cup rice vinegar

¹/₄ cup packed chopped fresh cilantro

2 tablespoons packed chopped fresh mint

1 tablespoon kosher salt

Position a rack on the top level of the oven, about 4 inches from the broiler. Turn on the broiler. Line a rimmed baking sheet with aluminum foil. Place the tomato halves, cut side down; the onion slices; and the chile on the prepared baking sheet and broil for about 10 to 12 minutes, or until the vegetables are soft and a bit charred. Let cool to room temperature.

In a food processor, combine the roasted vegetables and any juices from the pan with the vinegar, cilantro, mint, and salt and pulse until the mixture is almost, but not quite, smooth. If necessary, add up to ¹/₄ cup water to achieve a consistency similar to that of a thick soup. Taste and adjust the seasoning as necessary.

Serve now or store in an airtight container in the refrigerator for up to 3 days.

To puree or to chop, that is the question

At the restaurant, we go through so much of this salsa that pureeing it in a food processor is the only way to make enough. But it's fun to play around with the texture of just about any salsa. At home, try processing your salsas less or more for a chunkier or smoother result. Or, if you're not making a huge batch, try skipping the food processor altogether, get out the cutting board and chopping knife, and go old-school. A roughly chopped salsa has a completely different personality from a pureed one.

Tomatillo-avocado salsa

MAKES ABOUT 2 CUPS

5 tomatillos, husks removed

1 Hass avocado

1/2 jalapeño chile, stemmed and seeded

1 clove garlic, coarsely chopped

1/4 cup loosely packed chopped fresh cilantro

3/4 teaspoon ground cumin seeds

2 teaspoons freshly squeezed lime juice

2 teaspoons kosher salt

Husking tomatillos: a quick trick

To remove the husks from tomatillos, soak them in a bowl of warm water to cover for about 3 minutes. The husks should slip right off. Removing the husks this way also keeps your fingers from getting sticky.

One of the standard offerings in our Tacolicious trio of salsas, this mild and creamy avocado-based concoction is even popular with kids. Half of the tomatillos are roasted to give the salsa a smoky flavor, and the other half are kept fresh to deliver a zing. We prefer to use Hass avocados, which are as rich as butter. Every jalapeño has a different amount of heat, so if you're aiming for a mild salsa, taste the chile before you decide how much to add. Half of a jalapeño gives it just a bit of heat. Try this versatile salsa with the Potato and homemade chorizo taco (page 105), Spring booty taco (page 133), or Baja-style fish taco (page 139). But honestly, it goes well with most everything.

Position a rack on the top level of the oven, about 4 inches from the broiler. Turn on the broiler. Line a rimmed baking sheet with aluminum foil. Place 3 of the tomatillos on the prepared baking sheet and broil for 10 to 12 minutes, or until slighty charred and softened. Let cool to room temperature.

Slice the avocado in half, remove the pit, and scoop the flesh into a small bowl. Mash roughly with a fork and measure out 3/4 cup. Reserve the remainder for another use.

When the tomatillos have cooled completely, combine the 2 remaining fresh tomatillos and the roasted tomatillos in a blender with the avocado, chile, garlic, cilantro, cumin, and lime juice and puree on high speed for about 20 seconds, until completely smooth. Add the salt and process until blended. The salsa should be thick enough to have body but thin enough to pour. If necessary, adjust with a little cold water. Taste and adjust with more salt if needed.

Serve now or store in an airtight container in the refrigerator for up to 2 days.

Just-hot-enough habanero salsa

The color of sunshine (thanks to a not-so-secret-anymore dash of ground turmeric), this smooth, slightly sweet and floral salsa is one of the trio that we serve with our tacos at the restaurant. Although it has the most heat of the three, it's not so spicy that you're running to dunk your head in cold milk. In other words, you can actually savor it. You need only a drizzle of it to get results, which means this recipe makes more than enough for a single meal. We love spooning it over our Off-the-spit pork al pastor taco (page 121) and Cochinita pibil taco (page 126). The recipe will work if you cut it in half, but the salsa will be a bit more difficult to blend.

Heat the oil in a saucepan over medium-low heat. Add the onion, chiles, garlic, and salt (the salt can help keep the onion from taking on any color, which helps the salsa keep its clean, bright color) and cook, stirring frequently, for about 20 minutes, until the onion is soft and almost translucent.

Add the turmeric, vinegar, and water, increase the heat to bring the mixture to a boil, and then turn down the heat to a simmer and cook for 5 minutes. Remove the pan from the heat, let cool slightly, and pour the contents into a blender. Add the lime juice, turn on the blender to low speed, and then very gradually increase the speed to high until the salsa is the consistency of a smooth liquid. Taste and adjust with more salt if needed.

Let cool completely before serving, or store in an airtight container in the refrigerator for up to 4 days.

MAKES ABOUT 1½ CUPS

2 tablespoons vegetable oil

1 medium yellow onion, thinly sliced

4 habanero chiles, stemmed and coarsely chopped

2 small cloves garlic, coarsely chopped

1 tablespoon kosher salt

1 teaspoon ground turmeric

¼ cup rice vinegar

½ cup water

3 tablespoons freshly squeezed lime juice

The tale of the "very cute bell pepper"

Once upon a time, a friend of ours was grocery shopping with her small daughter, who loved nothing more than a good bell pepper. Struck by one particularly cheerful, bright orange, and irresistibly cute doll-size pepper, she asked her mother if she could bring it home as a treat. (Clearly, any kid that thinks a bell pepper is a treat is a keeper.) Our friend—a doting mother—said "sure!" But when they got home, her daughter took one bite and, well, let's just say it wasn't pretty. The moral of this story: know your habanero. And please don't feed it to your kids!

Lazy salsa, two ways

MAKES ABOUT 3 CUPS
FRESH OR
2 CUPS ROASTED

Fresh Lazy Salsa

4 Roma tomatoes, chopped

¹/₂ large yellow onion, finely chopped

1 jalapeño chile, stemmed and finely chopped

¹/₄ cup freshly squeezed lime juice

2 tablespoons chopped fresh cilantro

2 teaspoons kosher salt

Roasted Lazy Salsa

4 Roma tomatoes, halved lengthwise

¹/₂ large yellow onion, sliced into ¹/₂-inch-thick rounds

2 jalapeño chiles, stemmed

¹/₄ cup freshly squeezed lime juice (about 2 limes)

2 tablespoons chopped fresh cilantro

2 teaspoons kosher salt

What some know as *pico de gallo*, *salsa mexicana*, or *salsa fresca* (uncooked salsa) we prefer to call it by its other common, and very astute, name, *salsa huevona* or "lazy salsa." This easy-to-make classic salsa doesn't call for roasting or a blender and can be used on anything from eggs in the morning to grilled chicken at dinnertime. The only thing not to be lazy about is choosing good, ripe, in-season tomatoes. When the tomatoes aren't stellar, you can roast the vegetables, a method that requires a bit more get-up-and-go. Of course this is a classic chip dip, but try it with grilled meats and fish.

To make the fresh salsa, in a bowl, combine all of the ingredients and toss well. Taste and adjust the seasoning with salt if needed. Let sit for 15 minutes before serving. The salsa can be stored in an airtight container in the refrigerator for up to 2 days, but we think it tastes best the day it is made.

To make the roasted salsa, position a rack on the top level of the oven, about 4 inches from the broiler. Turn on the broiler. Line a rimmed baking sheet with aluminum foil. Place the tomato halves, cut side down; the onion slices; and the chiles on the prepared baking sheet and broil for about 10 to 12 minutes, or until softened and slightly charred. Let cool to room temperature.

In a food processor, combine the roasted vegetables and any juices from the pan with the lime juice, cilantro, and salt and pulse a few times until you have a nice chunky salsa. Taste and adjust the seasoning with salt if needed. For a more rustic texture, chop the roasted vegetables by hand and stir in the lime juice, cilantro, and salt.

Serve now or store in an airtight container in the refrigerator for up to 3 days.

Smoky chipotle–tomatillo salsa

This salsa doubles down on the chipotles: dried chipotles give it an extra smoky flavor, which is balanced by the tangy and sweet side of chipotles in adobo. The tomatillos function like tomatoes here, giving the salsa a necessary acidity. This is a great sauce for grilled red meats such as steak or lamb—or anything that can stand up to its boldness. Try it with the Carnitas taco (page 124) and the Potato and homemade chorizo taco (page 105), too.

MAKES ABOUT 1½ CUPS

1 tablespoon vegetable oil

2 dried chipotle chiles

½ cup water

4 tomatillos, husks removed

½ large yellow onion, sliced into ½-inch-thick rounds

3 cloves garlic

1 tablespoon freshly squeezed lime juice

¼ cup packed chopped fresh cilantro

1 tablespoon drained, coarsely chopped chipotle chile in adobo sauce

1 tablespoon cider vinegar

1 tablespoon kosher salt

Position a rack on the top level of the oven, about 4 inches from the broiler. Turn on the broiler. Line a rimmed baking sheet with aluminum foil.

Heat the oil in a skillet over medium heat. Add the dried chipotles and toast them, turning them several times, for 2 to 3 minutes, until they are toasted and start to puff up. Take care that they do not burn.

Transfer the chiles to a small bowl, add the water, and place another small bowl on top of the chiles to keep them submerged. Set the chiles aside to soften.

Place the tomatillos, onion, and garlic on the prepared baking sheet and broil for about 10 to 12 minutes, or until softened and slightly charred. (If the garlic threatens to burn before the other vegetables are ready, remove the cloves and let the tomatillos and onion continue to cook.) Set the vegetables aside to cool slightly.

Stem the softened chiles, reserving the soaking water. In a blender, combine the partially cooled vegetables and the softened chipotles and their soaking water with the lime juice, cilantro, chipotle in adobo sauce, vinegar, and salt and pulse until you have a salsa that still has a bit of texture.

Let cool completely before serving, or store in an airtight container in the refrigerator for up to 4 days.

Grilled tomato-habanero salsa

Influenced by the salsas of the Yucatán, this chunky, smoky, spicy blend is perfect for a summertime cookout or for any occasion for which you fire up the grill—particularly a charcoal grill. If you're really craving this salsa but don't have a grill available, don't be afraid to broil the vegetables for 10 to 12 minutes. Be forewarned, however, that without the grill, the smoky quality is diminished. One habanero makes this salsa plenty spicy, but you can crank up the heat with two. Spoon it over the Cheater's panucho (page 70), or try it with grilled chicken or fish.

Prepare a hot fire for indirect-heat cooking in a grill. Place the tomatoes, onion slices, and chile(s) on the grill rack away from the heat and grill, turning them as needed to char evenly, for 3 to 5 minutes on each side, until lightly charred and blistered. Set the vegetables aside to cool slightly.

In a food processor, combine the partially cooled vegetables with the lime juice, garlic, honey, and salt and pulse until the salsa has a chunky consistency. Taste and adjust the seasoning with salt if needed.

Serve now or store in an airtight container in the refrigerator for up to 3 days.

MAKES 2 TO 2$^1/_2$ CUPS

4 Roma tomatoes

1 small red onion, thickly sliced

1 or 2 habanero chiles, stemmed

$^1/_4$ cup freshly squeezed lime juice

1 small clove garlic, minced

1 teaspoon honey

1$^1/_2$ teaspoons kosher salt

Guajillo chile salsa

The heat level of this habit-forming smoky-sweet salsa is warming but not incendiary. Made up of nothing more than guajillo chiles and garlic, with a splash of vinegar for brightness, it is glossy, brick red, intensely flavored, and the perfect accompaniment to grilled red meats, yet equally tasty slathered onto *tortas*. Try it on tacos made of thinly sliced flank steak, Pickled red onions (page 41), and avocado slices. This salsa will keep for a long time, so the recipe is a good one to double. You'll discover that you don't need much of it to make a statement, either. Try making it with other dried chiles, such as tiny árbols or meaty anchos, for a different flavor and heat level.

MAKES ABOUT 1 CUP

2 ounces guajillo chiles (about 16), stemmed

3 large cloves garlic, unpeeled

1 cup hot water

2 tablespoons cider vinegar

1 teaspoon sugar

1 tablespoon kosher salt

Working in two batches to avoid crowding, lightly toast all of the chiles in a dry, heavy skillet over medium heat for 30 seconds on each side, until fragrant but not blackened. Transfer to a work surface and, when cool enough to handle, snip the chiles into 1-inch pieces with kitchen scissors to make them easier to blend. (The seeds are included in this recipe, so don't worry about trying to remove them.) Put the toasted chiles in a blender.

Add the garlic to the skillet and toast over medium-high heat, turning as needed, for 5 to 7 minutes, until the papery skin has blackened a bit and the flesh has started to soften. Let the cloves cool, then peel them and add them to the blender.

Add the hot water to the blender and let stand for about 5 minutes to allow the chiles and garlic to soften a bit. Now puree the mixture on high speed until smooth, adding a little more water if needed to achieve a slightly thick but soupy texture (in the end, the texture is up to you).

Transfer the mixture to a bowl and stir in the vinegar, sugar, and salt. Taste and adjust the seasoning, adding a bit more sugar or salt if needed. Because this is not a salsa you will use for dipping chips, it should be boldly flavored and a bit on the salty side.

Serve now or store in an airtight container in the refrigerator for up to 3 weeks.

The legendary orange sauce

This salsa is modeled after what is called nothing sexier than "the orange sauce" by the devoted regulars of La Victoria taqueria in San Jose, California. Because Telmo spent the better part of his young culinary life trying to perfect his own version, it was with some reluctance that he is sharing his recipe here. Although it is indeed creamy, this recipe contains no cream—only oil, which is emulsified to give the salsa a silky taste and texture. You'll find this sauce served in tiny squeeze bottles at Mosto, our tequila bar in San Francisco, where people squirt it generously over our street-size *tacos al pastor*. But it's the kind of salsa that makes just about everything taste better. This recipe makes quite a bit, but it will keep for a long time in your refrigerator, or you can bottle it and gift it to your most deserving friends.

Position a rack on the top level of the oven, about 4 inches from the broiler. Turn on the broiler. Line a rimmed baking sheet with aluminum foil. Place the tomatoes, cut side down, and the onion slices on the prepared baking sheet and broil for 10 to 12 minutes, until soft and a bit charred. Let cool to room temperature.

Heat 2 tablespoons of the vegetable oil in a sauté pan over medium-high heat. When the oil is hot, add the garlic and cook, turning the cloves several times with tongs, for about 3 minutes, until browned. Now add the chiles and heat them, turning them a few times, for 1 to 2 minutes, until they just start to toast. Take care that they do not burn. You want them to darken where they touch the pan but not blacken completely.

Transfer the chiles and garlic to a blender, pour in the vinegar and water, and let stand for about 5 minutes to soften. Add the roasted vegetables and any juice from the pan and the salt and puree on high speed until smooth.

Turn down the blender speed to low and pour the remaining $^7/_8$ cup oil through the small opening in the lid, adding it in a slow, steady stream. This ensures the mixture will emulsify, creating the desired creamy consistency. The end result should be slightly thick.

Serve now or store in an airtight container in the refrigerator for up to 2 weeks.

MAKES ABOUT 3 CUPS

2 Roma tomatoes, halved lengthwise

$^1/_2$ yellow onion, sliced into $^1/_2$-inch-thick rounds

1 cup vegetable oil

3 large cloves garlic

$^1/_2$ cup packed dried árbol chiles, stemmed

$^1/_3$ cup cider vinegar

$^1/_2$ cup water

1 tablespoon kosher salt

Cal-Mex corn salsa with tomatoes and basil

MAKES ABOUT 4 CUPS

1¹/₂ cups fresh corn kernels (from about 3 ears)

1¹/₂ cups chopped ripe tomatoes

1 cup diced, unpeeled English cucumber

1 tablespoon finely chopped, seeded jalapeño chile

¹/₂ cup finely chopped red onion

1 tablespoon freshly squeezed lime juice

¹/₂ cup loosely packed chopped fresh basil

2 teaspoons kosher salt

With far more of a Californian accent than a Mexican one, this mild fresh salsa is a bit of a misfit in the company of the others. But it's so delicious that it had to be included. It demands ripe tomatoes and crunchy, sweet corn, which means it's best made at the height of summer. Cilantro would make a good substitute for the basil, or try adding some chopped fresh mint or tarragon. We like it with shrimp cakes (page 63), but it is also a great salsa with roasted chicken or grilled salmon, spooned atop chicken soup with rice, or scooped up with chips. To make this salsa even prettier, remove the seeds and pulp from the tomatoes before chopping them.

In a bowl, combine all of the ingredients, toss and stir to mix well, and let sit for 15 minutes to marry the flavors. Taste and adjust the seasoning with salt if needed.

The salsa tastes best served the day it is made, but it can be stored in an airtight container in the refrigerator for up to 1 day.

Cumin-lime crema

A lighter and more flavorful alternative to regular *crema*, or Mexican sour cream, this thick, cumin-spiked cream will brighten up just about any dish that you would top with sour cream or plain yogurt. At Tacolicious, we use it on our Baja-style crispy fish tacos and on our fried plantains with refried beans, but try it tossed with ripe tomatoes, chilled cucumbers, and cilantro for a refreshing summer salad. Alternatively, pair it with some of our other tacos, such as the Potato and homemade chorizo taco (page 105); Butternut squash, kale, and crunchy pepitas taco (page 144); Tangy achiote-rubbed grilled chicken taco (page 134); Lone Star breakfast taco (page 143); or Spring booty taco (page 133).

Toast the cumin in a small dry, heavy skillet over medium heat for about 1 minute, until its aroma hits your nose. Transfer to a spice grinder, let cool, then grind finely.

In a ceramic or glass bowl, whisk together the yogurt, sour cream, ground cumin, and salt. Using a zester, grate the zest of the limes directly into the bowl. Add the lime juice and whisk until well combined. Taste and adjust the seasoning with salt if needed.

Serve now or store in an airtight container in the refrigerator for up to 4 days.

MAKES ABOUT 2 CUPS

2 teaspoons cumin seeds

1 cup plain yogurt

1 cup sour cream

2 teaspoons kosher salt

Zest of 2 limes

4 teaspoons freshly squeezed lime juice

El Jefe's glove-box recado

Like some sort of drug dealer, Joe (aka the big boss) has been known to keep a small plastic bag of this addictive Mexican spice rub in his glove box. And indeed, it's never a bad thing to have on hand. Although the recipe has a few steps to it, it's well worth the effort. At the restaurant, we use it to season everything from corn on the cob (page 57) to chicken to our Spring booty taco (page 133). When cooking with it, just beware that it's quite salty. Also, it keeps for a long time, which means that you may want to make a double batch.

(page 57)
(page 133)

MAKES ABOUT 1¹/₂ CUPS

2 tablespoons vegetable oil

3 ancho chiles, stemmed and seeded

3 dried chipotle chiles, stemmed and seeded

2 tablespoons dried Mexican oregano

15 cloves garlic, chopped

³/₄ cup kosher salt

Line a plate with a paper towel. Heat the oil in a heavy skillet over medium heat. When the oil is hot, add the ancho chiles and fry, turning once, for about 1 minute on each side, until puffy and crispy. Be careful they do not to burn. Transfer the anchos to the paper-lined plate to drain. Repeat with the chipotle chiles. Let the chiles cool completely.

Toast the oregano in a small, dry skillet over medium heat, shaking the pan frequently to prevent burning, for about 1 minute, until fragrant. Let cool completely.

Transfer the ancho chiles to a spice grinder, grind to a powder, and transfer to a small bowl. Repeat with the chipotle chiles, followed by the oregano. (If you cannot fit the chiles into your spice grinder, grind them in the food processor in the next step.)

In a food processor, combine the garlic, salt, ground oregano, and ground chiles and process until the mix has a fine, grainy, sandy consistency similar to that of coffee grounds. If the mixture is damp, turn on the oven to the lowest setting, spread the mixture on a baking sheet, and place the pan in the oven until the mixture dries out, stirring it every 10 minutes. Alternatively, spread the mixture on the baking sheet and let it sit out overnight at room temperature, stirring it a few times. Use now or store in an airtight container at room temperature for up to1 month.

Four more ways to use this recado

1. Make chorizo by adding 1 tablespoon *recado* to 1 pound ground pork shoulder. Mix well and shape into patties to grill or panfry.

2. Rub a whole chicken with the *recado* before roasting it in a 400°F oven until done.

3. Lightly season raw shrimp in the shell with tail segments intact with the *recado* (taking care, as the *recado* is very salty) and a squeeze of lime juice and let marinate for 30 minutes. Thread onto a skewer and grill.

4. Beat together eggs with a bit of *crema*. Mix in a pinch of *recado* for a bit of salty, smoky heat. In a pan over medium-low heat, scramble the egg mixture. Top with cilantro and serve in a tortilla.

Tamarind-habanero glaze

We use this sweet, spicy, tangy glaze like a Mexican barbecue sauce, tossing our tender baby back pork ribs in it (page 83). But chicken wings in the style of buffalo wings would also be awesome, as would a big spoonful stirred into a pot of beans. The tamarind (look for it in puree, concentrate, or paste form), which gives this glaze its pucker power, is available at Latin, Southeast Asian, and Indian markets, though some gourmet markets carry it, as well. The number of habaneros you use is up to your heat tolerance. Two are definitely for the spicy at heart.

Put all of the ingredients in a blender and puree on high speed for about 30 seconds, until smooth.

Pour the puree into a saucepan over medium-low heat and simmer uncovered, stirring now and again, for about 25 minutes, until thickened to a glaze consistency. Take note that it will thicken as it cools.

Let cool to room temperature before using. It will keep in an airtight container in the refrigerator for up to 2 weeks.

MAKES ABOUT 2 CUPS

1 cup ketchup

1 cup tamarind puree

1 tablespoon finely chopped garlic

$^{1}/_{4}$ cup honey

$^{1}/_{3}$ cup freshly squeezed orange juice

2 tablespoons Worcestershire sauce

3 tablespoons rice vinegar

1 or 2 habanero chiles, stemmed

$1^{1}/_{2}$ tablespoons kosher salt

Pickled red onions

A staple in the Yucatán, these sweet-and-sour onions are found on everything from *cochinita pibil* (page 126) to fish tacos to *panuchos*. Place them on the table as a condiment just like salsa. Truly, no taco is better off without them.

Put the onions in a large, heatproof glass or ceramic bowl.

Combine the vinegar, water, oregano, sugar, and salt in a saucepan and bring to a boil over medium-high heat. Remove from the heat immediately and pour over the onions. Cover the bowl with plastic wrap and let sit for at least 6 hours before using.

The onions can be stored in an airtight container in the refrigerator for up to 1 week.

MAKES ABOUT 2 CUPS

2 cups sliced red onions (in half-moons)

1 cup rice vinegar

1 cup water

$1^{1}/_{2}$ tablespoons dried Mexican oregano

2 tablespoons dark brown sugar

2 tablespoons kosher salt

Pickled cauliflower, carrots, and jalapeños

MAKES ABOUT 2 CUPS

1 cup small cauliflower florets

1 cup thinly sliced, peeled carrots (in $1/8$-inch-thick coins)

$1/2$ cup sliced red onion (halved and cut lengthwise into $1/2$-inch-thick slices)

$1^1/2$ cups sliced jalapeño chiles (in $1/4$-inch-thick rounds)

1 cup rice vinegar

1 cup water

2 tablespoons sugar

2 tablespoons kosher salt

6 whole cloves

1 tablespoon dried Mexican oregano

1 bay leaf

2 large cloves garlic, lightly crushed

When it comes to setting the table in Mexico, this mix of spicy pickled vegetables, also known as *escabeche*, is almost as expected as salsa. At Tacolicious, we include cauliflower, but most typically you'll see jalapeños, carrots, and onions. Unless you have the time and the desire, don't worry about removing the seeds from the chiles. Try experimenting with a chunkier version, too, leaving the jalapeños whole and cutting the carrots into large pieces.

Put the cauliflower, carrots, onion, and chiles in a wide-mouthed quart canning jar or a heatproof glass or ceramic bowl.

Combine the vinegar, water, sugar, salt, cloves, oregano, bay leaf, and garlic in a saucepan and bring to a boil over high heat. Remove from the heat. Place the jar or bowl in your sink to catch any overflow and carefully pour the vinegar mixture over the vegetables. Let sit for about 1 hour, or until completely cooled.

If you have used a jar, screw on the lid. If you have used a bowl, transfer the vegetables and liquid to a plastic container with a tight-fitting lid. Let sit at room temperature for 24 hours before serving. The vegetables will keep in the refrigerator for up to 1 month.

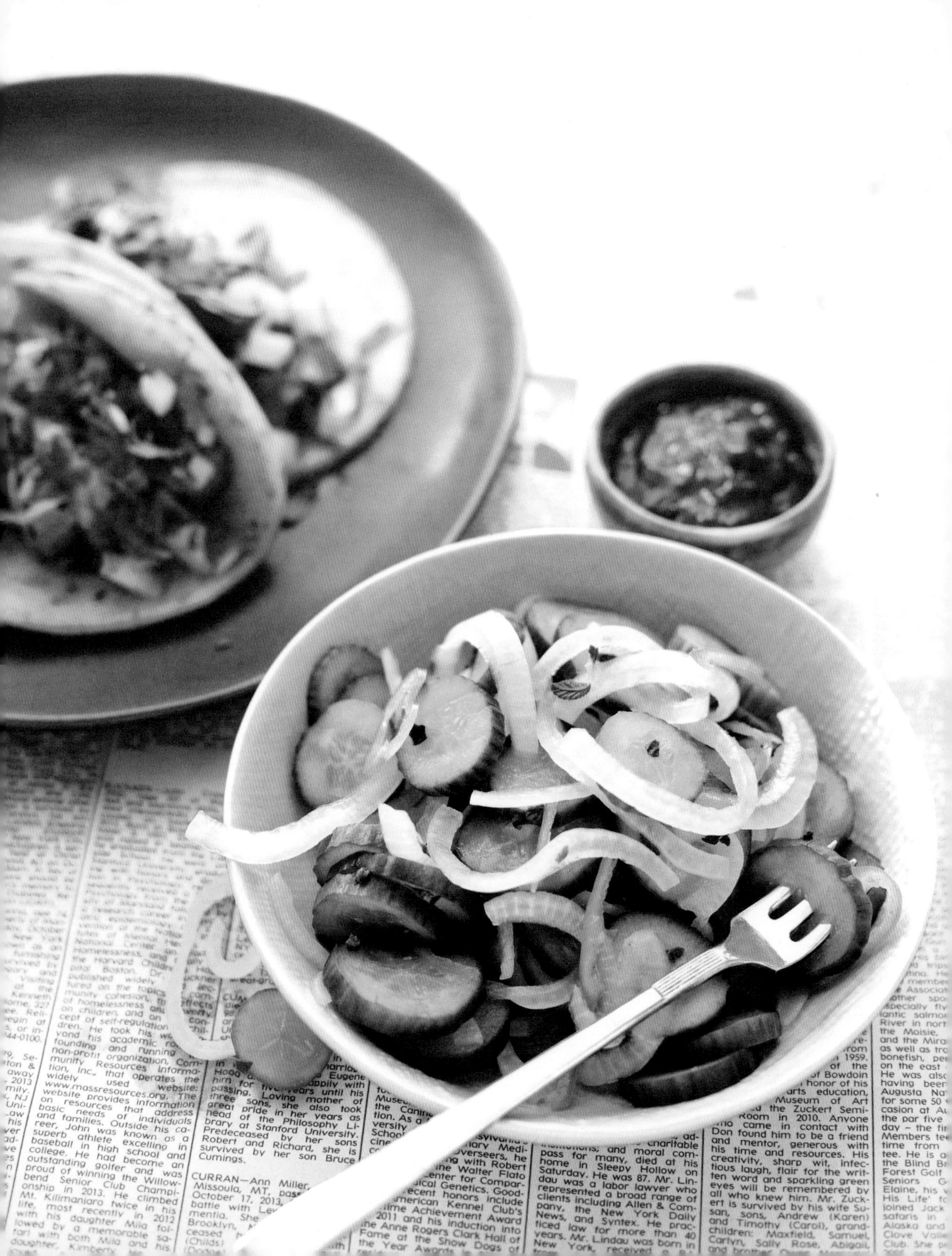

Lime-cured cucumber, habanero, and onion

At Contramar in Mexico City (see more gushing about this fantastic restaurant on page 13), a variation on this devilish concoction might seem simple, but it gives pretty much anything you add it to an electrifying pop. Try it with fried dishes like fish tacos or meats such as braised pork. As you might imagine, it cuts straight to the chase and isn't for the faint of heart.

Combine all of the ingredients in a glass or ceramic bowl and let rest for 1 to 2 hours, stirring every 30 minutes or so.

Serve now or store in an airtight container in the refrigerator for up to 2 days, though the spiciness will increase as time passes.

1 yellow onion, halved crosswise and sliced into $1/8$-inch-thick half-moons

1 English cucumber, halved lengthwise, seeded, and cut crosswise into $1/8$-inch-thick half-moons

1 habanero chile, stemmed, seeded, and sliced crosswise paper-thin

$1/4$ cup freshly squeezed lime juice

1 teaspoon dried Mexican oregano

1 teaspoon kosher salt

snacks
+ sides

47

Botanas, a sexier-sounding Spanish word for the term *appetizers*, generally refers to snacky things, the kind of noncommittal dishes that you might set out in the vicinity of a cocktail: the type of food that makes people happy. *Antojitos*, or "little cravings," fit effortlessly into the *botanas* category. These *masa-* or corn tortilla–based two- or three-bite dishes, generally born on the streets of Mexico, embrace, yes, tacos, but also tamales, tostadas, quesadillas, and *tortas*.

This chapter includes all of the above—except tacos, which get their own chapter. Much of what you will find here is finger food, from a party mix of pumpkin seeds and peanuts for serving with a beer and a shot of tequila to little tostadas smeared with black beans and topped with shredded turkey and cabbage that your kids will eat up. On the other side of the spectrum, you'll find bracing ceviches: one dotted with capers and citrus that's elegant enough to serve at a dinner party and another that is a more casual *aguachile* meant for scooping up with chips.

Although this chapter offers more than enough to put together a satisfying menu, it's also meant to help enhance any level of taco fiesta. A summer cookout is elevated with a platter of watermelon and mango,

dressed with chile powder and salt and a squeeze of lemon (a classic salty-spicy-sweet Mexican combination), or with grilled corn on the cob rubbed with an addictive chile-based *recado*. When it's cold outside, you're going to want to turn to a comforting bowl of *albóndigas* in chipotle sauce. Seasonal affective disorder can easily be cured by dipping into a warm bowl of *chile con queso* (though, like drinking, it's addictive and best not to indulge in alone).

Whatever the occasion, the following recipes are here to help get the party started.

Chupitos: the appetizer of cocktails

This chapter of snacks and sides is full of appetizer-size bites of food—little nibbles whose main purpose is to rev up the taste buds. At Tacolicious, we sell shot-size glasses of cocktails, called *chupitos*, which serve the same purpose. To make *chupitos* at home, simply shake up one of the cocktails from the final chapter (starting on page 171) and pour it, chilled, into tall shot glasses (skip the ice). It's a great way for your guests to sample a few cocktails without having to commit to one. Think of it as a liquid hors d'ouevre.

Mexican party mix

From crispy *chicharrónes* to crunchy fried favas, little salty snacks are served in every decent bar in Mexico. This is our personal favorite, peanuts and pumpkin seeds. Instead of frying them (though that's definitely a delicious option), we roast them in the oven, which makes them both easy to make and guilt free to eat.

MAKES ABOUT 4 CUPS

2 tablespoons freshly squeezed lime juice

2 tablespoons sugar

2 cups shelled raw pumpkin seeds

2 cups unsalted roasted peanuts

1¹/₂ teaspoons sweet paprika

1 teaspoon cayenne pepper

1 teaspoon freshly ground black pepper

1 tablespoon kosher salt

Preheat the oven to 350°F.

Combine the lime juice and sugar in a large glass or ceramic bowl and microwave on high for 30 to 60 seconds, until the sugar has dissolved and a syrup forms. (Alternatively, combine the lime juice and sugar in a small saucepan and heat over medium heat until the sugar has dissolved, then transfer to a large bowl and let cool.)

Add the pumpkin and peanuts seeds to the bowl with the lime syrup, and toss until the nuts and seeds are thoroughly coated. In a small bowl, stir together the paprika, cayenne, black pepper, and salt. While stirring constantly, evenly sprinkle the spice mix over the nuts and seeds.

Line a rimmed baking sheet with parchment paper or rub with vegetable oil. Spread the seasoned seeds and nuts on the prepared pan and roast for 15 to 20 minutes. Stir a couple of times while roasting, taking care not to let the nuts burn. Transfer to a serving bowl and serve warm or at room temperature.

The party mix will keep in an airtight container at room temperature for up to 1 week.

The Mex-Americana version: just add Chex Mix

If you want to go for an Americana take on this Mexican bar snack, try adding 2 cups of Chex cereals (any mix of corn, rice, and wheat flavors) and 1 cup of small pretzels and bumping up the amount of spice mix a bit. This is a more healthful alternative to the traditional middle-American version, which calls for a ton of butter.

Chile con queso

It took our good friend Mike Harden, an Arkansas native raised on "cheese dip," as it's called there, to open our eyes to the addictive qualities—we're talking twelve-step-program kind of addictive—of *chile con queso*. Of course, our righteous San Francisco ways compelled us to try out all sorts of other, more natural cheeses first, but we finally caved to the sumptuous beauty of Velveeta, a shelf-stable cheese that's so wrong yet so right. In the same vein, canned green chiles and tomatoes are integral to the goodness of the dish. (Though, should you have some of our homemade *escabeche* [page 42] around, the jalapeños make a great replacement for the traditional store-bought pickled chiles.) Today, our *chile con queso* isn't just popular with the masses, but is also a favorite of a local Michelin-starred chef. In other words, if you like it as much as we do, you're in good company. You can make it up to 2 days in advance and reheat it in the microwave or in a small pot over low heat.

MAKES ABOUT 4 CUPS

1 tablespoon vegetable oil

1/2 yellow onion, chopped

1 teaspoon minced garlic

1 pound Velveeta cheese, cut into 2-inch cubes

1 (7-ounce) can Ortega brand diced green chiles, drained

3/4 cup diced canned tomatoes with juice

1/4 cup drained canned or jarred sliced pickled jalapeño chiles

Tortilla chips, for dipping

Combine the oil, onion, and garlic in a saucepan over medium heat and cook until the onion is translucent, about 5 minutes. Add the cheese and stir frequently until melted. Add the green chiles, tomatoes, and pickled jalapeños and stir until heated through.

Transfer to a serving bowl and serve warm with tortilla chips for dipping.

Four-star nachos

This book holds the key to making the ultimate nachos. First, you need good-quality, not-too-salty chips with some integrity to them, topped with a good drizzle of our Chile con queso. For a vegetarian version that no meat eater will pass up, top with Not really refried beans (page 92), Pickled red onions (page 41), Classic guacamole (page 53), Cumin-lime crema (page 37), Roasted tomato–mint salsa (page 24), and a shower of chopped fresh cilantro. For a carnivore's delight, add any one of the braised meats, such as Shot-and-a-beer braised chicken (page 132). Serve with cold beer and lots of napkins.

Classic guacamole

In both Mexico and California, the regular consumption of avocados is like a birthright. Yes, these buttery fruits are fatty, but luckily, their monounsaturated fat is good for you. We make our guacamole to order at the restaurant, and you should, too. The flavor is brighter, and the color stays true. Although the recipe that we follow at Tacolicious calls for a bit of our Tomatillo-avocado salsa (page 26), this one doesn't. The result is still great with fewer steps. Guacamole should not be relegated to chips only. Pile it on tacos, spread it on sandwiches, or use it as a dip for vegetables. To mash the avocado, simply scoop the flesh into a bowl and take a fork to it. You're not going for baby food, so leave it a bit chunky.

Place the avocado in a bowl. Add the garlic, onion, chile, cumin, lime juice, cilantro, and salt and use a fork to smash everything together to your desired consistency. Taste and adjust with salt or lime juice if needed.

Let sit for about 15 minutes before serving to allow the flavors to come together.

MAKES 2 HEAPING CUPS

2 cups gently mashed avocado, preferably Hass (from about 4 avocados)

$1/2$ teaspoon minced garlic

2 tablespoons diced yellow onion

1 tablespoon minced jalapeño chile

$1/4$ teaspoon ground cumin

$1^1/2$ tablespoons freshly squeezed lime juice

2 tablespoons chopped fresh cilantro

$1^1/4$ teaspoons kosher salt

The secret to the perfectly ripe avocado

Avocados are always harvested unripe and allowed to ripen at room temperature. Thus, purchasing them hard and letting them soften at home is the best way to avoid bruised specimens. To speed the ripening process, place the immature avocados in a paper bag with an apple or a banana. If you need immediate satisfaction, select avocados that have a bit of give to them. Don't let the produce vendor see you gently pressing your thumb into an avocado, however. Do it on the sly or face a scolding.

Melon, mango, and cucumber with chile, salt, and lime

One of the hallmarks of Mexican cuisine is the flavor combination of salty, spicy, sour, and sweet. It extends from sweets and candies to fresh fruit. In the streets, vendors sell bags of sliced fruit and cucumbers topped with salt, chile powder, and a big squeeze of lemon or lime juice. The following instructions are so simple that they barely qualify as a recipe. Success here is all about finding the best fruit available. Look for Kent mangoes. Big and green, they slice open to reveal the sweetest, most ambrosial flesh. For another presentation, try doing as the street vendors do and slice your fruit and cucumber into spears (pictured) rather than cubes. Serve the spears plunked upright into tall glasses, so people can pick them up with their fingers.

SERVES 4 TO 6

1 small, ripe melon (such as cantaloupe, seedless watermelon, or honeydew), chilled

2 ripe Kent or other large mangoes, or 3 ripe Manila or other small mangoes

1 English cucumber, chilled

2 tablespoons kosher salt

2 tablespoons chile powder of your choice

2 or 3 limes, halved

To prepare the melon, cut it in half. If it has a seed cavity, scoop out and discard the seeds. Cut the rind away from the flesh, and then cut the flesh into 1-inch cubes.

To prepare the mangoes, hold a mango on one of its narrow edges, with the stem facing you. Position a sharp knife just to the right of the stem end (or to the left of it if left-handed) and cut downward, running your knife as closely as possible to the pit. Repeat on the opposite side of the pit. Using a paring knife, peel away the skin from each mango "cheek," then slice the flesh into 1-inch cubes.

To prepare the cucumber, cut it in half lengthwise, then cut each half lengthwise in half again. Cut crosswise into 1-inch cubes.

Put the cubed melon, mango, and cucumber in a large bowl, sprinkle with the salt and chile powder, and toss to coat evenly. Taste and adjust with more salt or chile powder if needed.

Serve in little bowls with the lime halves for squeezing in juice as desired.

Grilled corn on the cob with glove-box recado

Chilly as July and August can be in San Francisco, you know it's summer when this delicious corn hits the Tacolicious menu. (It is so good that it transports you to sunshine, even if the city is socked in by fog and you're wearing a scarf.) If you already have the *recado* ready to go, this recipe is a cinch to make. Although the smokiness of the grill imparts great flavor, you can instead briefly boil the corn ears, halve them, and toss them with the *recado*–lime juice mixture. With the lime and the spices, no butter is needed. Try swapping out the corn for another vegetable, such as summer squash. To keep this recipe in the snack realm, chop the ears into thirds.

Prepare a medium-hot fire for direct-heat cooking in a grill. Place the ears of corn on the grill rack and grill, turning them as needed to color evenly, for 10 minutes, until they have a bit of char to them but haven't cooked so much that the kernels have wrinkled. You want to maintain the sweet, fresh corn crunch. Remove from the grill and cut in half crosswise.

In a large bowl, mix together the *recado* and lime juice. Add the corn and toss until evenly coated. Take a bite of one ear and adjust the remaining ears with more *recado* and lime juice to taste. Serve hot.

SERVES 4

4 ears corn, shucked and silk removed

2 tablespoons El Jefe's glove-box recado (page 38), plus more if needed

1 tablespoon freshly squeezed lime juice, plus more if needed

Donnie's halibut crudo with citrus and capers

1 pound sushi-grade skinned halibut or other firm, mild white fish fillet

6 tablespoons extra virgin olive oil

$^1/_4$ cup freshly squeezed lime juice

2 tablespoons rice vinegar

$^1/_2$ serrano chile, sliced crosswise paper-thin

1 shallot, minced

$^1/_2$ teaspoon agave nectar

Kosher salt and freshly ground black pepper

Light green inner leaves of 1 head celery

2 oranges, peeled, sectioned, and seeded

2 small Ruby Red or other red grapefruits, peeled, sectioned, and seeded

1 tablespoon drained capers

2 tablespoons coarsely chopped fresh flat-leaf parsley

2 tablespoons coarsely chopped fresh mint

2 tablespoons coarsely chopped fresh basil

4 radishes, thinly sliced

Coarse sea salt, for garnish

Our good friend and talented chef Donnie Masterton has long lived and worked in San Miguel de Allende, one of Mexico's most beautiful colonial towns, where he owns a place called The Restaurant. When we want additional inspiration, we give Donnie a call, which is exactly how we acquired this beauty of a recipe. Don't cheap out with the olive oil. In fact, if you can find olive oil infused with orange or other citrus, pick up a bottle to use. Try swapping the grapefruits for blood oranges for another gorgeous presentation.

Cut the fish into pieces about $^1/_8$ inch thick, 1 inch wide, and 2 inches long.

Stir together the oil, lime juice, and vinegar in a bowl. Add the chile, shallot, and agave nectar, season with kosher salt and pepper, and stir to mix. Add the fish, toss gently to coat evenly, and let sit for about 5 minutes.

Place the celery leaves along the middle of a long serving platter. Alternate the orange and grapefruit sections around the celery, reserving some fruit for garnish.

Using a slotted spoon, lift the fish from the dressing and arrange the pieces on top of the celery leaves. Spoon the dressing over the fish and sprinkle with the capers, parsley, mint, basil, and radishes. Garnish with the reserved citrus sections, sprinkle with the sea salt, and serve.

A summer's night shrimp cocktail

Telmo grew up in a Mexican neighborhood in San Jose, California. On warm evenings, he could be found at a busy roadside seafood joint called La Costa spooning up refreshing bites of *coctel de camarón*, or "shrimp cocktail." Served in a tall Styrofoam cup, the La Costa cocktail combines a sweet (but not cloying), tangy, and spicy tomato-based sauce, briny poached shrimp, avocado, cucumber, and *pico de gallo*, all topped with some shakes of a *salsa picante* and served with tostadas or saltine crackers. Our version is made with roasted fresh tomatoes instead of the traditional ketchup to brighten it up. The resulting sauce is more like a gazpacho than the typical country club–style cocktail sauce. The cocktail can be assembled a couple of hours ahead of time, but not too far in advance, as the shrimp becomes rubbery if left in the lime juice for too long. To make this shrimp cocktail into easy party fare, spoon it onto small store-bought tostadas, garnish with a little cilantro, and serve.

Position a rack on the top level of the oven, about 4 inches from the broiler. Turn on the broiler. Line a rimmed baking sheet with aluminum foil. Place the tomato halves on it, cut side down. Broil for 10 to 12 minutes, or until the tomatoes are softened and slightly charred. Allow to cool to room temperature.

Combine 4 quarts of the water, 1/4 cup of the lime juice, and 2 tablespoons salt in a large saucepan and bring to a boil over high heat. Add the shrimp and cook for about 3 minutes, until they are fully cooked. They should be bright pink-orange, curled, and firm but not hard. Immediately drain the shrimp into a colander and hold under running cold water for about 1 minute. Drain well, transfer to a bowl, cover, and refrigerate until cold.

To make the cocktail sauce, combine the roasted tomatoes, the remaining 1/2 cup water, the remaining 2 tablespoons lime juice, the adobo sauce, the honey, the garlic, the Worcestershire sauce, and the pepper in a blender and puree on high speed until smooth. Season to taste with salt.

Pour the sauce into a large ceramic or glass bowl. Add the shrimp, avocado, cucumber, onion, diced tomato, cilantro, and jalapeño. Stir gently to mix.

Serve in tall glasses or sundae glasses with long spoons and accompany with the crackers. Pass the lime wedges at the table.

3 Roma tomatoes, halved lengthwise, plus 1/4 cup seeded and diced ripe tomato

4 quarts plus 1/2 cup water

1/4 cup plus 2 tablespoons freshly squeezed lime juice

Kosher salt

1 1/2 pounds medium-size shrimp, tails removed, peeled, and deveined

2 tablespoons sauce from chipotle chiles in adobo sauce

1 1/2 tablespoons honey

1 small clove garlic, minced

1 teaspoon Worcestershire sauce

Pinch of freshly ground black pepper

1 avocado, halved, pitted, peeled, and cubed

1/2 cup cubed unpeeled English cucumber

1/4 cup chopped yellow onion

1/4 cup loosely packed chopped fresh cilantro

1 tablespoon minced jalapeño chile (optional)

Saltine crackers, for serving

Lime wedges, for serving

Aquachile with avocado and cucumber

SERVES 6

1 pound sushi-grade firm, mild fish fillet (such as halibut, mahimahi, or snapper), skinned and cut into ¹/₂-inch cubes

³/₄ cup freshly squeezed lime juice (from about 6 juicy limes), plus 2 tablespoons

1 cup loosely packed chopped fresh cilantro, plus ¹/₄ cup chopped for garnish

3 tablespoons chopped fresh mint

1 small clove garlic, coarsely chopped

1 tablespoon vegetable oil

2 tablespoons water

1 tablespoon kosher salt

³/₄ cup ¹/₄-inch-cubed, unpeeled English cucumber

³/₄ cup ¹/₄-inch-cubed slightly firm avocado

¹/₂ cup chopped red onion

¹/₂ to 1 habanero chile, stemmed and finely chopped

Tortilla chips, for serving

This is our take on *aquachile,* a type of Mexican ceviche most commonly prepared by dousing raw shrimp with a bracing bath of lime juice, herbs, and chiles and serving it soon thereafter. Present this version in individual bowls spiked with a few tortilla chips for scooping. Fried plantain chips would be good, too.

Combine the fish and the ³/₄ cup lime juice in a glass or ceramic bowl and toss to coat the fish evenly. Cover with plastic wrap and refrigerate, stirring the fish a couple of times to ensure it is always coated with lime juice, for 30 minutes, until the fish starts to turn opaque.

Meanwhile, in a blender, combine the 1 cup cilantro with the mint, garlic, oil, remaining 2 tablespoons lime juice, water, and salt and puree until combined.

Drain the lime juice from the fish. Add the cilantro puree to the fish and toss to coat well. Add the cucumber, avocado, onion, and half of the chile and toss gently to mix. The flavor should be bracing—tart, nicely salty, and spicy. Add more chile if desired.

Divide among individual bowls, sprinkle evenly with the remaining ¹/₄ cup cilantro, and serve immediately. Accompany with the chips.

So many fish in the sea: variations on aguachile

Although the *aguachile* recipe calls for a mild fish, it is really just a template. Experiment with other seafood, such as scallops or peeled and deveined shrimp. Mix up your selection of herbs (try basil or even a bit of shiso), or consider cranking up the amount of chile or using jalapeño or serrano instead of habanero (though we like the floral notes of a habanero). The only requisite is that you use perfectly fresh seafood and plenty of lime to quickly "cook" it.

Shrimp cakes with corn-basil salsa

Here is a perfect warm-weather dish to pass at a party or serve as a sit-down appetizer. If you don't want to go through the hassle of making your own chipotle aioli, mix 3 tablespoons mayonnaise and 1 tablespoon sauce from chipotle chiles in adobo sauce.

MAKES ABOUT 12 CAKES;
SERVES 4 TO 6

Place the shrimp in a food processor and pulse just until some small chunks of shrimp remain. Transfer the shrimp to a bowl. Add the egg, lime juice, chipotle aioli, chopped celery, green onions, parsley, celery salt, paprika, salt, pepper, and 1 cup of the panko. Pour the remaining 1½ cups panko into a shallow bowl.

Line a baking sheet with parchment or waxed paper. Using your hands, form the shrimp mixture into patties each about 2 inches in diameter and about ½ inch thick. They should barely hold together or they will cook up tough. One at a time, gingerly place the patties in the panko and then turn to coat the other side. As each patty is coated, place it on the prepared baking sheet. Cover the baking sheet with plastic wrap and refrigerate for at least 30 minutes or up to 1 day.

Heat 2 tablespoons of the oil in a large cast-iron or other heavy skillet over medium-low heat. When the oil is hot, add half of the cakes, making sure not to crowd them. Cook the cakes, flipping them once, for about 3 minutes on each side, until golden brown. Transfer the finished cakes to a plate and set aside (in a 250°F oven if you aren't serving them immediately). Add the remaining 2 tablespoons oil to the skillet and cook the remaining cakes the same way.

Serve the shrimp cakes topped with a spoonful of salsa.

Try it with salmon

Shrimp are great, but if you're lucky enough to have in-season local wild salmon around—blindingly and beautifully colored—it would make a great substitute. Unfortunately, wild salmon has become heart-wrenchingly expensive. But turning its rich meat into a little cake is a perfectly thrifty way to have your salmon and eat it, too. Increase the amount of panko if the mixture seems to require more to bind into patties. (Equally expensive crabmeat is the other obvious substitute.)

1½ pounds medium-size shrimp, tails removed, peeled and deveined

1 egg, lightly beaten

1 tablespoon plus 2 teaspoons freshly squeezed lime juice

¼ cup chipotle aioli (see Tuna tostadas, Contramar style, page 66)

⅓ cup finely chopped celery (about 1 small stalk)

⅓ cup finely chopped green onion, green part only (about 3 onions)

⅓ cup loosely packed finely chopped fresh flat-leaf parsley

½ teaspoon celery salt

1½ teaspoons sweet paprika

1 teaspoon kosher salt

½ teaspoon freshly ground black pepper

2½ cups panko (Japanese bread crumbs)

4 tablespoons vegetable oil

2 cups Cal-Mex corn salsa with tomatoes and basil (page 36)

The ultimate torta

One of our favorite places to eat in San Francisco is a little place called La Torta Gorda in the Mission District. (Not coincidentally, it's a block away from La Palma [see page 123], the place that makes our tortillas.) At La Torta Gorda, owner Armando Macuil serves up perfect *tortas* as well as items like quesadillas with squash blossoms and *huitlacoche* (a delicious, good-for-you corn fungus) that are traditionally found in the state of Puebla, Mexico, where he grew up. La Torta boasts a little patio out back, and on a warm day, we sit there and order a toasty, oozy *pierna enchilada torta* (pulled-pork sandwich, our personal favorite) and a nopal-and-pineapple *agua fresca*, and life seems to be in perfect working order.

A *torta* might seem like just a sandwich, but to anyone who knows better, it is an art. Just for us, Armando gave up some of his secrets.

Three steps to a perfect torta

1. First you need to get the right bread. Although in Mexican bakeries you can find variations on the *bolillo*, a crunchy bread modeled after the French baguette, look for rolls of *talera*, which is distinctive because it's slightly softer, a bit flatter, and has three shallow slashes in it.

2. To make a *torta*, slice the *talera* in half lengthwise and add a swipe of refried pinto beans, a couple of slices of good-quality, moist *queso fresco* (best purchased at a Latin market), a few avocado slices and red onion slices, a scattering of pickled jalapeños (page 42), and the meat of your choice. The key is to restrain yourself from including too much of each ingredient. You aren't looking to make a huge, honking sandwich. Everything should be in harmony.

3. Cook the *torta* in a panini press for 3 minutes, until just a bit toasty. Alternatively, place on a *comal* (flat, round, or oblong griddle) or cast-iron skillet, cook until crisp on the first side, and turn to toast the other side.

Torta filling inspiration

Just like any sandwich, the combinations are infinite, but here are some fillings that would work perfectly. You can count on any braised meat to be a winner. And definitely serve the *torta* with a salsa or two for dipping or for spreading.

Guajillo-braised beef short rib (page 102)

Shot-and-a-beer braised chicken (page 132)

Cochinita pibil (page 126)

Potato and homemade chorizo (page 105)

Lamb adobo (page 118)

Carnitas (page 124)

Albóndigas in tomato-chipotle sauce (page 80)

Nopal, egg, and tomato (page 147)

Q + A with Armando

Is there any secret to a perfect *torta*?

"You have to have good ingredients, and the perfect amount of them—just a thin layer of each. Most places add lettuce, tomato, and sour cream, but we don't because when you take a bite, everything comes out."

What are your favorite *torta* fillings?

"Milanese de pollo (thinly pounded, breaded, and fried chicken fillet), pulled pork, a cubana (hot dogs plus the kitchen sink), jamón, and pambazo (a classic from Puebla and Mexico City made with potato and chorizo). The pambazo is the only one that we make with lettuce and sour cream. It's dipped in an adobo sauce, then put on a griddle. I also like chorizo and egg tortas for breakfast."

Where do you find the best *tortas* in Mexico?

In the markets. I used to get mine at Torta Tony's in the tianguis (open-air bazaar) in Puebla, where you can buy everything from socks to shorts to chickens to cows and cars. The market opens at 2:00 a.m. At 5:00 a.m., I'd have my first torta of the day. And then another one at noon.

Tuna tostadas, Contramar style

The first time we dined at Contramar, Mexico City's lauded seafood restaurant, we had an awakening. Suddenly Mexican food wasn't just the delicious, homey, "authentic" food of our previous travels (*authentic* being a nebulous word at best), but something sophisticated yet casual, urban, and exciting. And this signature dish of Contramar's—a heavenly fusion of Asian and Mexican—is the ultimate example of that. To get it right, we even flew Telmo down to DF to stage (the culinary term for *intern*) in the Contramar kitchen. *See photos on pages 68–69.*

See photos on pages 68–69.

MAKES 12 TOSTADAS; SERVES 6

Chipotle Aioli

1 egg yolk, chilled

1 tablespoon freshly squeezed lemon juice

1 clove garlic, minced

1/2 cup vegetable oil

1/4 cup drained, chopped chipotle chiles in adobo sauce

1 teaspoon kosher salt

Tostadas

Vegetable oil, for deep-frying

12 (4- to 5-inch) corn tortillas (purchased this size or cut to size with scissors)

To make the aioli, combine the egg yolk, lemon juice, and garlic in a blender and blend for 30 to 45 seconds, until smooth. With the blender running, pour in the oil in a very slow, thin, steady stream until the mixture emulsifies and thickens. (If the aioli begins to break, try alternating the oil with drops of ice water until the mixture has emulsified.) Add the chiles and salt and process for an additional 30 seconds, until the chiles are fully incorporated. Transfer to a covered container and refrigerate until needed; it will keep for up to 3 days.

To make the tostadas, pour the oil to a depth of 1 inch into a large, deep, heavy skillet and heat to 375°F on a deep-frying thermometer. Line a large plate with paper towels. Add the tortillas, one or two at a time (depending on the size of the pan), to the hot oil and cook, turning once with tongs, for 1 to 1 1/2 minutes on each side, until a uniformly deep golden color and crisp. Transfer to the towel-lined plate to absorb the excess oil. Fry the remaining tortillas the same way. Set aside.

Remove the pan from the heat, reserving the oil in the pan to fry the leeks.

Put the leeks and just enough water to cover in a small saucepan and bring to a boil over high heat. Remove from the heat, drain into a colander, and place under cold running water for about 30 seconds, until completely cool. Press gently on the leeks to remove any excess water, then press between paper towels to wick away excess moisture.

Line a small plate with paper towels. If the tortillas have absorbed some of the oil in the skillet, add more oil until it is again 1 inch deep. Place the skillet over medium-low heat and heat the oil to 325°F. Carefully add the leeks to the hot oil and fry, stirring once about halfway through the frying, for about 5 minutes, until golden brown and crispy but still a little green. Be careful not to let them burn. Using a slotted spoon, transfer the leeks to the towel-lined plate to drain.

Stir together the soy sauce and lime juice in a glass or ceramic bowl. Add the tuna slices and stir gently, coating all of slices with the marinade. Let marinate for 5 minutes, then pour off the excess marinade.

To assemble the tostadas, place the tostadas on a flat work surface and spread about 2 teaspoons of the chipotle aioli on each tostada. Place 3 tuna slices on top of the aioli, then top each portion of tuna with about 2 teaspoons of the leeks. Finally, top each tostada with 2 avocado slices, then season the avocado with a tiny pinch of salt.

Serve the tostadas immediately, accompanied with the lime wedges.

3 large leeks, white and light green part only, halved lengthwise, then cut crosswise into 1/4-inch-thick half-moons (3 cups)

1/2 cup soy sauce

1/2 cup freshly squeezed lime juice (from about 4 limes)

1 pound sashimi-grade skinned tuna fillet, cut into 1/8-inch-thick slices

2 avocados, halved, pitted, peeled, and cut into 24 slices each 1/8 inch thick

Kosher salt

12 lime wedges (about 2 limes)

Two quick but dignified tuna tostada shortcuts

Followed to a tee, this recipe for tuna tostadas has quite a few steps. Luckily, it also has a couple of optional shortcuts.

1. Although the flavor will not be as fresh, buy premade tostadas. The only caveat is that smaller tostadas, which we highly recommend for this appetizer, can be difficult to source.

2. To make an easy, down-and-dirty chipotle mayo, stir sauce from chipotle chiles in adobo sauce to taste into store-bought mayonnaise.

Tuna tostadas,
Contramar style, page 66

Cheater's panucho

**MAKES 12 PANUCHOS;
SERVES 4 TO 6**

Turkey

**2 tablespoons
achiote paste**

**1/2 cup unsweetened
pineapple juice**

**1/2 cup freshly squeezed
lime juice (from about
4 limes)**

1/2 cup water

**4 cloves garlic,
coarsely chopped**

2 teaspoons kosher salt

**1/2 teaspoon dried
Mexican oregano**

**1/4 teaspoon ground
allspice**

**2 pounds bone-in turkey
thighs, skin removed**

Panuchos are one of the Yucatán's rightful claims to fame. To make these addictive *antojitos*, thick, freshly made tortillas are griddled until they puff up enough to form little pitalike pockets, which are stuffed with refried black beans. They are then deep-fried and topped with slow-cooked achiote-marinated chicken or turkey (which, if you are being traditional, you wrapped in banana leaves and cooked in an earthen oven), chopped cabbage, tomato, avocado, and pickled onions. So, yes, this much easier recipe isn't really a *panucho*. It's an inspired tostada with all the proper fixings. Serve with our Just-hot-enough habanero salsa (page 27). To keep it super simple, we suggest you purchase pre-made tostadas. (But if you want to make your own, follow the directions from the Tuna tostadas, Contramar style recipe [page 66].) To make it even easier, use prepared, canned refried black beans.

To make the turkey, combine the achiote paste, pineapple juice, lime juice, water, garlic, salt, oregano, and allspice in a blender and puree until a smooth sauce forms. Pour into a saucepan.

Bring the sauce to a boil over medium-high heat, turn down the heat to a simmer, and add the turkey. Cover partially and braise for 1 1/2 to 2 hours, until the turkey can be easily shredded. Remove the turkey from the sauce, reserving the sauce, and allow the turkey to cool. Using your fingers, pull the meat from bones, discarding the bones, and finely shred it. Place in a bowl, add 1 cup of the reserved sauce, and set aside.

To make the beans, heat the oil in a skillet over medium heat. Add the onion and garlic and sauté for about 3 minutes, until softened. Add the black beans, salt, and cumin and cook, stirring occasionally, for 5 minutes, to heat through and blend the flavors. Remove from the heat, transfer to a food processor, allow to cool slightly, then pulse until a creamy paste forms. Transfer to a bowl, taste then adjust the seasoning, and set aside.

Rinse the food processor bowl. Slice the cabbage into wide strips, transfer to the food processor, and pulse until finely chopped. Measure out 2 cups and set aside. Reserve any excess for another use.

To assemble the *panuchos*, spread a thin layer of the black bean puree onto each tostada. Top with a bit of shredded turkey, some chopped cabbage, a tomato slice, a slice or two of avocado, and a few slices of pickled onion. The idea is not to overload the tostada but rather have a small bit of everything. Serve immediately.

Tulum: where panucho dreams are made

The beautiful, laid-back beach town of Tulum is where Joe and I have found our *panucho* heaven. When we visit we return over and over to El Rinón Chiapaneco, a little open-air spot frequented by both locals and visitors that makes, to our mind, the ultimate *panucho*. There's something perfect about their kitchen's judicious, slim ratio of tortilla to black beans to shredded turkey to sliced tomato, avocado, and cabbage (which they chop to the point of looking like snow), and a few pickled onions. We always each order three *panuchos*, which we enjoy with a cold beer or a *jugo verde*, a blend of *chaya* (a leafy green vegetable) and pineapple juice.

Refried Black Beans

2 tablespoons vegetable oil

$1/2$ cup chopped yellow onion

1 tablespoon chopped garlic

1 (15-ounce) can black beans, drained and rinsed

1 teaspoon kosher salt

$1/2$ teaspoon ground cumin

$1/4$ head green cabbage

12 (4- to 5-inch) tostadas

12 slices ripe tomato

12 to 24 slices avocado

2 cup Pickled red onions (page 41)

Quesadillas with squash blossoms, sweet peppers, and goat cheese

SERVES 6

12 small sweet or gypsy peppers, halved lengthwise and seeded

4 tablespoons vegetable oil

1 cup sliced yellow onion (halved lengthwise, then sliced into half-moons)

4 ounces squash blossoms (about 24), stemmed and coarsely chopped, stamens and all

1 tablespoon finely chopped fresh mint

2 teaspoons kosher salt

6 corn tortillas

¹/₄ cup shredded Oaxaca cheese

¹/₄ cup fresh goat cheese

Squash blossoms are most easily found at farmers' markets, specialty produce markets, or, if you're a gardener, in your own backyard. (Harvesting your own blossoms is one good way to curb a bumper crop of zucchini.) Small, delicate, multicolored peppers sold under the general name "mini sweet peppers" have become a popular option at gourmet supermarkets. If you can't find them, substitute meatier red or yellow bell peppers, similarly roasted and then cut into strips.

Position a rack on the top level of the oven and preheat the broiler. Place the peppers, cut side down, on a rimmed baking sheet and broil for 5 to 10 minutes, until slightly charred and softened. Remove from the oven and slice the peppers lengthwise into strips ¹/₂-inch wide.

Heat 2 tablespoons of the oil in a heavy skillet over medium heat. Add the onion and sauté for about 3 minutes, until softened. Add the squash blossoms and peppers and sauté for 5 minutes more, until the peppers are softened. Add the mint and salt, stir to combine, and remove from the heat. Taste and adjust the seasoning with more salt if needed.

Wipe out the skillet, add 1 teaspoon of the oil, and place over medium heat. Place a tortilla in the skillet and cook for 15 to 30 seconds, until softened and toasty smelling. Place a spoonful of the filling (about one-sixth of the total) in the center. Sprinkle with a little Oaxaca cheese, top with a few dots of goat cheese, and fold the tortilla in half. Allow to cook for a few seconds longer, then flip the tortilla and cook on the second side until the cheese is fully melted. Transfer to a plate. Repeat with the remaining oil, tortillas, squash mixture, and cheeses.

Will the real quesadilla please stand up?

For Americans, quesadillas are like the Mexican equivalent of a grilled cheese sandwich: flour tortillas filled with cheese and then toasted on a griddle until oozy. In Mexico, quesadillas are somewhat more sophisticated. Traditionally, they are made with fresh corn *masa* (dough) that is pressed into a round, filled, and then sealed like a little turnover and deep-fried or toasted on a *comal* (griddle). This recipe is a quesadilla hybrid.

Flaky potato-and-greens empanadas with salsa verde

Made with a flaky, buttery dough, these empanadas are completely addictive and well worth the work. Although this recipe is vegetarian, you could replace the filling with Guajillo-braised beef short rib (page 102) or Shot-and-a-beer braised chicken (page 132). You can also add different herbs or greens. (Just make sure the filling isn't too juicy or it will seep out as the empanadas bake, so use a slotted spoon as needed.) You can make the dough up to 2 days in advance. If you're plating the empanadas, try spooning the *salsa verde* (or any salsa) over them and topping them with a bit of Cotija cheese, slices of avocado, chopped cilantro and onion, and a drizzle of *crema*.

To make the salsa, in a blender, combine the tomatillos, onion, garlic, chiles, cilantro, and salt and puree until almost smooth. Place a saucepan over medium heat, add the oil, and allow to heat for a few seconds. Pour the salsa into the pan (very carefully because it will splatter) and cook, stirring frequently, for about 15 minutes, until reduced by half. You should have about 1 cup. Set aside to cool.

To make the dough, stir together the flour and salt in a large bowl. Scatter the butter over the flour and then work the butter into the flour with a fork or with your fingers until the mixture has an even, coarse texture. The lumps of butter should be no larger than the size of a pea.

In a small bowl, whisk the eggs until blended, then whisk in the water and vinegar. Using your hands or a fork, slowly mix the egg mixture into the flour mixture until thoroughly blended, being careful not to overwork the dough or it will be tough. The dough should look a bit shaggy. Cover the bowl with plastic wrap and set aside in a cool spot to rest for 1 hour.

Shape the dough into twenty-four 2-inch balls, arrange on a tray or large platter, cover with plastic wrap, and refrigerate until needed.

MAKES 24 EMPANADAS

Salsa Verde

1 pound tomatillos, husks removed and chopped

1/2 cup chopped yellow onion

6 cloves garlic, coarsely chopped

3 tablespoons finely chopped, seeded jalapeño chile

1/4 cup loosely packed chopped fresh cilantro

1 teaspoon kosher salt

3 tablespoons vegetable oil

Dough

4 cups all-purpose flour

4 teaspoons kosher salt

1 1/2 cups cold unsalted butter, cut into 1-inch pieces

2 eggs

2/3 cup water

4 teaspoons white vinegar

Continued

Continued

Flaky potato-and-greens empanadas with salsa verde

Filling

2 tablespoons vegetable oil

1 cup finely chopped yellow onion

1 tablespoon finely chopped garlic

1 pound fingerling or Yukon gold potatoes, cut into 1/2-inch cubes

1 cup finely chopped Swiss chard

1 tablespoon finely chopped fresh oregano

1/4 cup water

1 teaspoon kosher salt

Pinch of freshly ground black pepper

1 1/4 cups shredded Oaxaca cheese

To make the filling, heat the oil in a large skillet over medium heat. Add the onion and garlic and sauté for 3 to 5 minutes, until softened. Add the potatoes and continue to cook, stirring occasionally, for 5 to 7 minutes, until nearly soft. Add the chard, oregano, and water and cook, stirring occasionally, for about 2 minutes, until the chard is wilted. Add the salt and pepper, stir well, and remove from the heat. Let cool completely, then mix in the cheese. Set aside.

To assemble the empanadas, remove half of the dough balls from the refrigerator and let them sit for a few minutes to warm up a bit. Flour a work surface and a rolling pin, place a ball on the floured surface, and roll out into a round 4 1/2 inches in diameter and 1/8 inch thick. Repeat with the remaining 11 balls, then remove the remaining balls from the refrigerator and repeat the process. You should have 24 dough rounds.

Spoon about 2 heaping tablespoons of the filling evenly on one half of a round, leaving a 1/2-inch border. Fold the uncovered half over the filling, to form a half-moon. Using the tines of a fork, crimp and press the edges together, sealing them closed. (Alternatively, for a more professional look, press the edges together with a fingertip, then finish with a pastry fluter.) To ensure the seal, you can dab the inside of the border with a little water before folding over the round. Repeat with the remaining rounds and filling. Cover the empanadas with plastic wrap and chill for at least 1 hour or up to 1 day before baking.

Preheat the oven to 450°F. Line a large rimmed baking sheet with parchment paper.

Arrange the empanadas on the lined baking sheet, spacing them about 2 inches apart. Bake for 10 to 15 minutes, until golden brown.

Serve the empanadas warm, accompanied with the salsa for dipping or for spooning over the top.

Freezer to table: a neat trick

To freeze the assembled empanadas before baking, arrange them in a single layer on a tray or baking sheet, place in the freezer until frozen solid, then transfer to one or more zippered plastic freezer bags and freeze for up to a month. Then, when you are ready to bake, arrange the empanadas, still frozen, on a parchment paper–lined baking sheet and bake as directed, increasing the baking time to about 20 minutes.

Ms. Reyes's most awesome tamales

When we were opening our first brick-and-mortar Tacolicious, our good friend Saul Peña came by the construction site with a bunch of his mother's Salvadoran tamales to sustain us. Wrapped in banana leaves, they married silken, broth-infused *masa* with a stuffing of chicken, potatoes, and green beans and were, hands down, the best tamales we'd ever tasted. Today we serve Ms. Reyes's tamales at our tequila bar Mosto. Although the recipe calls for many steps, they can blessedly be done in stages. Once it's time to assemble, call on a few friends to help out and make a little party out of it. You can make the tamales themselves up to a week in advance or freeze them. By using a vegetable broth and stuffing them with sweet potatoes and greens, we've even made them vegan with great success. Unprepared *masa* is moist corn dough (without any addition of salt, lard, or broth) and can be found at some Mexican markets and *tortillerias*. Don't confuse it with the *masa harina*, which is dried ground corn sold in bags on the shelves. A tamale is only as good as its *masa*, so make sure it's fresh without any sour aroma.

Combine the water and 3 tablespoons salt in a large pot and bring to a boil over high heat. Add the chicken and turn down the heat to medium-high to keep the water at a gentle boil. After 15 minutes, add the tomatoes, celery, carrot, onion, bell pepper, and bay leaf. Turn down the heat to a simmer and cook, uncovered, for about 1 hour, until a drumstick easily pulls away from a thigh.

Remove the pot from the heat, lift out the chicken legs, and set aside. Strain the liquid through a fine-mesh sieve and set the stock aside, reserving it for later. Pick out and discard the bay leaf from the sieve and set the vegetables aside. When the chicken is cool enough to handle, discard the skin and bones and shred the meat. Put the meat in a bowl and set aside.

Put the chiles in a bowl, add hot water to cover, top the chiles with a weight to keep them submerged, and let soak for about 15 minutes, until softened.

Remove the chiles from their soaking water and put them in a blender along with a few tablespoons of the water and the reserved cooked vegetables. Process until a smooth sauce forms. Add one-third of the sauce to the chicken meat and toss to coat. Taste and adjust the seasoning with salt if needed. Set

MAKES 24 TAMALES

12 cups water

Kosher salt

1³/₄ pounds whole chicken legs (about 3)

2 Roma tomatoes

1 celery stalk, halved crosswise

1 carrot, peeled and halved crosswise

¹/₂ yellow onion

¹/₂ red bell pepper, seeded

1 bay leaf

2 guajillo chiles, stemmed

5 ounces green beans, cut into 2-inch pieces

1 large russet potato, peeled and cut into ³/₄-inch cubes

2 pounds finely ground fresh masa

24 (9 by 8-inch) banana-leaf rectangles (from about 2 pounds; see sidebar on page 79)

Salsa of choice, for serving (optional)

Continued

Continued

Ms. Reyes's most awesome tamales

the remaining chile-vegetable sauce and the chicken aside. At this point, the chicken and sauce can be refrigerated for up to 2 days before completing the tamales.

Bring a saucepan filled with water to a boil over high heat. Salt the water liberally, add the green beans, and cook for about 2 minutes, until crisp-tender. Using a slotted spoon, transfer the beans to a bowl. When the water returns to a rapid boil, add the potato and cook for about 3 minutes, until not quite cooked through. Drain and set aside in a separate bowl.

Pour the reserved stock into a large pot, place over medium heat, and add the reserved chile-vegetable sauce. When the stock is simmering, place a fine-mesh sieve over the pot and add the masa to the broth, using a spoon to press it through the sieve, whisking as you go. Then whisk in 2 teaspoons salt.

Now, whisk continuously for about 20 minutes (yes, your arm will hurt), until the mixture is thick and smooth. It should have an almost puddinglike consistency reminiscent of creamy polenta. Remove from the heat.

To assemble the tamales, use scissors to cut out twenty-four 10 by 9-inch parchment-paper rectangles. (See banana leaf tips on page 79.) Place 1/2 cup of the hot prepared *masa* in the middle of a banana-leaf rectangle and spread it into a 4 by 3-inch rectangle, lining it up with the grain of the leaf. Place about 2 tablespoons of the chicken, a few pieces of potato, and a few pieces of green bean on top of the *masa*. Make a 1/2-inch fold on each long side of the leaf. Bring these sides together over the filling so that they overlap a bit, as if you were wrapping a present. Flip the tamale over and fold the right and left sides over the bottom of the tamale. Flip the tamale over once again. Wrap the tamale in parchment paper the same way you wrapped it in the banana leaf. Repeat until you have used all of the *masa* and filling. (If you are unable to master folding the tamale into a Martha Stewart–perfect little package, don't worry. The most important thing is to enclose the filling securely.)

Arrange the tamales in a steamer basket or an Asian-style bamboo steamer (you can pile them on top of one another in a couple of layers) and place over water in a pot. Cover the pot, bring the water to a boil, adjust the heat to maintain a simmer, and cook for 45 minutes to 1 hour, until the *masa* is fully cooked through, but still tender. To check whether the tamales are ready, carefully unwrap one.

Serve the tamales with your favorite salsa, or eat them plain as they do in El Salvador, where spicy food isn't their thing.

Thoughts on wrangling the fierce banana leaf

Although banana leaf–wrapped tamales are sometimes simply tied with a bit of banana leaf, Ms. Reyes wraps them for a second time in parchment paper, which helps secure the *masa* and saves the day when a banana leaf is cracked—a frustrating inevitability.

In fact, banana leaves are so fickle that it's best to buy more than you need so that you can toss out any pieces that get too many rips. You will find them in Latin and Asian groceries (see page 200 for more information).

It is a good idea to heat the banana leaves to make them more pliable, which can even be done a day ahead of assembling the tamales. To do this, first cut the banana leaves into the desired size, then place each piece in a dry skillet set over medium-low heat for about 1 minute on each side, until the sheen has dulled and the leaf is pliable but not burned.

But our best tip? Remain calm in the face of banana-leaf adversity. Even if the banana leaves have a few little rips, your tamales will still taste great.

Albóndigas in tomato-chipotle sauce

MAKES ABOUT 20 LARGE
MEATBALLS; SERVES 6

Meatballs

1 pound ground beef

1 pound ground pork

1/2 yellow onion, finely chopped (about 1/2 cup)

1/2 cup finely crumbled queso fresco

1 Roma tomato, diced

1/4 cup long-grain white rice, rinsed

1/4 cup loosely packed chopped fresh mint

1/4 cup loosely packed chopped fresh cilantro

2 teaspoons minced garlic

2 eggs, whisked

2 tablespoons all-purpose flour

4 teaspoons kosher salt

Tomato-Chipotle Sauce

4 cups diced canned tomatoes with their juice

1/2 cup chipotle chiles in adobo sauce

2 tablespoons vegetable oil

1/2 yellow onion, finely chopped

1 tablespoon minced garlic

3 cups low-sodium chicken broth

2 tablespoons Worcestershire sauce

This recipe is based on Mexican tradition but rooted in cross-cultural comfort. We'd feel confident bragging to any Italian grandmother that you haven't had a meatball until you've had these. Big and tender, they're spiked with fresh mint and cilantro and served in a slightly spicy, smoky, brothy sauce made of tomatoes and chipotles. Accompany them with tortillas—corn or flour—for dipping. We like our meatballs big and beefy, but you can make them any size you want. Just adjust the cooking time accordingly. You don't want them to overcook, which is why you cook them only partially in the oven before adding them to the sauce. In a pinch, fresh ricotta, though moister, can work in place of the *queso fresco.*

Preheat the oven to 375°F. Oil 2 rimmed baking sheets.

To make the meatballs, in a large bowl, combine all of the ingredients and mix gently to blend evenly. Dampening your hands to lessen stickiness, roll the meat mixture between your palms into uniform meatballs, each about the size of a golf ball on steroids. You will need a generous 1/4 cup of the mixture for each meatball. As the balls are formed, place them on the prepared baking sheets, spacing them about 1 inch apart.

Roast the meatballs for 15 minutes, until they are about three-fourths of the way cooked through. They will continue to cook in the sauce. Remove from the oven and set aside. (This step can be done 1 day in advance. Let the meatballs cool, cover with plastic wrap, and refrigerate until needed.)

To make the sauce, in a blender, combine the tomatoes and chiles and puree until smooth. Set aside.

Heat the oil in a large saucepan over medium-low heat. Add the onion and garlic and sauté for about 5 minutes, until translucent. Add the tomato-chile mixture and cook for 5 minutes more to marry the flavors. Add the broth, Worcestershire sauce, sugar, salt, cumin, oregano, and pepper, bring to a simmer, turn down the heat to low, and cook gently, uncovered, for about 10 minutes. Taste and adjust the seasoning with salt if needed. (At this point, the sauce can be cooled, covered, and refrigerated for up to 1 day. Return the sauce to a simmer over low heat before continuing.)

Add the partially cooked meatballs to the sauce and simmer uncovered, stirring gently every now and again to ensure that all of the meatballs cook evenly in the sauce, for about 40 minutes, until the meatballs are cooked through but still moist. Test a meatball to make sure that the rice is fully cooked.

Transfer the meatballs and sauce to a serving bowl and garnish with the *queso fresco*. Serve with tortillas for scooping up the yummy sauce.

Go green: meatballs in salsa verde

Another way to serve meatballs is in the sauce used for *chile verde* (green sauce). To do this, make the meatballs and roast them until partially cooked as directed. Then turn to page 129 for Mama Virginia's chile verde and make the sauce recipe as directed. Now, add the meatballs to the green sauce and simmer for about 40 minutes. This variation would also work well with ground turkey substituted for the beef and pork.

1 tablespoon dark brown sugar

1 tablespoon kosher salt

1 1/2 teaspoons ground cumin

1 1/2 teaspoons dried Mexican oregano

1/2 teaspoon freshly ground black pepper

Crumbled queso fresco, for garnish

Corn or flour tortillas, warmed (see page 108), for serving

Spicy tamarind-glazed pork ribs with jicama salad

With their addictive spicy, tangy glaze, cooled by a side of crisp jicama salad, these pork ribs are fiesta-ready. We serve them at our parties, but they would be just as at home as a starter at a more intimate sit-down dinner. This recipe has a few steps, so try to spread them out over a couple days. The glaze can be made and the ribs can be cooked a day ahead, leaving the crisping of the ribs to the last minute. Serve with extra napkins.

In a small bowl, stir together the salt and sugar, mixing well. Place the pork ribs in two 9 by 13-inch roasting pans, slicing between the bones as necessary to make the ribs fit. Divide the sugar-salt mixture in half and rub half on each rib rack, coating it entirely. Cover and refrigerate for 4 hours.

Position 2 racks in the center of the oven and preheat the oven to 325°F.

Carefully remove the rib rack from each pan, then divide the beer evenly between the pans, pouring it into the bottom. Return the rib racks to the pans, being careful not to lose any of the sugar-salt rub en route. Cover each pan with aluminum foil, place in the oven, and bake for about 2 1/4 hours, until the meat is tender and pulls away from the bone without too much difficulty.

Remove the ribs from the pans and let cool to room temperature. Once cool, cut the racks into single ribs by slicing lengthwise between the bones. Each rack should give you 12 or 13 ribs. (At this point, the ribs can be covered and refrigerated for up to 1 day, then brought to room temperature before continuing.)

To make the salad, combine the jicama, radishes, cilantro, and lime juice and toss to mix. Season with salt and toss again. Set aside while you finish the ribs.

If the tamarind glaze has been prepared in advance and refrigerated, bring it to room temperature.

Before you heat and crisp the ribs, make sure they are at room temperature. Position a rack in the oven 4 inches from the heat source and preheat the broiler. Arrange the ribs in a single layer on a rimmed baking sheet and place under the broiler. Broil the ribs, turning once, for several minutes on each side, until heated

SERVES 6
(ABOUT 4 RIBS EACH)

1/4 cup kosher salt

1/4 cup dark brown sugar

2 full racks pork baby back ribs (about 6 pounds total)

1 (12-ounce) bottle beer

1 1/4 cups Tamarind-habanero glaze (page 41)

Salad

3 cups sliced jicama, cut into 2 by 1/4-inch sticks (about 1 large jicama)

4 radishes, thinly sliced

1/2 cup loosely packed fresh cilantro leaves, coarsely chopped

1/4 cup freshly squeezed lime juice

Kosher salt

Continued

Spicy tamarind-glazed pork ribs with jicama salad

through and crisped. (Alternatively, for a smokier flavor, heat them on a hot charcoal grill until they start to char slightly.)

Transfer the ribs to a large bowl, pour the tamarind glaze over the top, and toss to coat well. Keep warm.

Serve the ribs with the jicama salad on the side.

The ultimate summertime party

The spirit of this soiree lies in top-notch seasonal ingredients and a smoking grill. Once the best, sweetest summertime corn and tomatoes hit the market, we often build a menu around them—we can't get enough of these warm-weather treats.

- Chips and Lazy salsa (page 28, fresh version)

- A summer's night shrimp cocktail (page 61)

- Grilled corn on the cob with glove-box recado (page 57)

- Spicy tamarind-glazed pork ribs with jicama salad (page 83, finished on the grill)

- Melon, mango, and cucumber with chile, salt, and lime (page 54)

La hamburguesa, DF style

In the restaurant industry, our R & D (research and development) trips should really be called E & D (eating and drinking) trips. And when we visit Mexico City, it often becomes mostly D—all in the name of business, of course. The next step is to mop up the tequila with a burger, which is sold from street stands. At Mosto, we serve up our version of a DF *hamburguesa*, which includes a juicy griddled beef patty, melty Oaxaca cheese, roasted poblanos (aka *rajas*), spicy serrano mayo, and pickled onions.

SERVES 6

2 pounds ground beef

2 poblano chiles

^{1}/$_2$ cup mayonnaise

1 teaspoon finely minced serrano chile

1 tablespoon kosher salt

Freshly ground black pepper

2 to 3 tablespoons vegetable oil

^{3}/$_4$ cup shredded Oaxaca or Monterey Jack cheese

6 good-quality hamburger buns, split

^{1}/$_2$ cup Pickled red onions (page 41)

Divide the ground beef into 6 equal portions. Form each portion into a ball and then press into a patty about ^{1}/$_2$ inch thick. Place the patties on a baking sheet or tray, cover with plastic wrap, and refrigerate until ready to cook.

Place the poblano chiles directly over the flame of a gas burner and turn with tongs for about 3 minutes, until charred and blistered all over. Alternatively, place the chiles in a dry, heavy skillet over high heat and turn with tongs for about 3 minutes, until charred and blistered all over. Transfer the chiles to a bowl, cover with plastic wrap, and let steam for 10 minutes. Remove the chiles from the bag and gently peel or scrape away the skin. Slice each chile in half lengthwise, remove the stem and seeds, and cut into strips (*rajas*) 1^1/$_2$ to 2 inches long and about ^{1}/$_4$ inch wide. Set aside.

Stir together the mayonnaise and serrano chile, cover, and refrigerate.

Remove the patties from the refrigerator. Season them on both sides with the salt and with pepper and let them rest for 10 minutes. Heat a griddle or large, heavy skillet over medium-high heat and add 1 tablespoon of the oil. When the oil is hot, add as many patties as will fit without crowding and cook for about 3 minutes on the first side, until browned on the underside. Flip the patties over, top each one with 2 tablespoons of the cheese and about 2 tablespoons of the poblano strips, and cook for about 4 minutes longer, until browned on the second side and done to your liking. Transfer the patties to a plate. Repeat the process with the remaining patties. Add 1 tablespoon oil to the pan before adding a new batch.

To assemble the burgers, spread each bun with the serrano mayonnaise. Place a burger and some pickled onions on top, and then close the bun. Serve immediately.

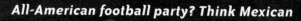

All-American football party? Think Mexican

Wings and potato skins are nice, but the following menu will spice up any Super Bowl party. It also suits a World Cup fiesta—celebrating that sport known as football in the rest of the world.

• Chips with Chile con queso (page 52)

• Classic guacamole (page 53) and carrot, celery, or other vegetable spears for dipping

• Mexican party mix (page 50)

• Bacon-wrapped hot dogs with jalapeño-cucumber relish (page 89)

• Michelada (page 182)

• Pitcher of Margarita picante (page 171)

• Alka-Seltzer (purchase at your nearest drugstore)

Bacon-wrapped hot dogs with jalapeño-cucumber relish

On any given night in San Francisco's Mission District—or Mexico City, for that matter—the aroma of bacon and griddled onions wafts from the many vendors slinging this classic street food. It beckons like a siren: you know eating it is going to cause you to crash into the rocky shore of caloric regret, but you go for it anyway. Don't use fancy thick-cut bacon for this one. Something like Original Oscar Meyer is best. At the restaurant, we add chopped roasted poblano chiles to the mayo, which makes a nice addition should you have the time.

To make the relish, in a food processor, combine the chiles, cucumber, and onion and chop finely, using about 10 quick pulses. Transfer to a heatproof bowl, mix in 1 tablespoon of the salt, and set aside.

To make the brine for the relish, combine the vinegar, sugar, garlic, peppercorns, allspice, cumin, coriander, star anise, cinnamon, bay leaves, and the remaining 1½ teaspoons salt in a small saucepan, place over low heat, and bring to a simmer. Cook for 15 minutes, then remove from the heat and strain through a fine-mesh sieve into the jalapeño-cucumber mixture. Cover and let cool.

In a small bowl, stir together the mayonnaise and the lime zest and juice. Cover and refrigerate until needed.

Wrap each hot dog with a bacon slice, circling the bacon around the hot dog and tucking each end of the bacon slice underneath the wrap to secure in place. Heat a large, heavy skillet over medium heat and (unless you have a huge pan or a griddle) add half of the bacon-wrapped hot dogs. Cook, turning the hot dogs as needed to ensure the bacon is crispy all over, for about 10 minutes. Transfer the hot dogs to a platter and, if desired, cover with foil and keep warm in a 250°F oven. Cook the remaining 5 hot dogs and add to the platter.

Drain off all but 2 tablespoons of the bacon fat from the pan and return the pan to medium-high heat. Add the onions and cook, stirring occasionally, for about 10 minutes, until lightly caramelized.

To assemble the hot dogs, smear a generous 2 tablespoons of the lime mayonnaise on each bun. Slip a hot dog into each bun, top with some relish and onions, and serve immediately.

SERVES 10

Relish

1 cup sliced jalapeño chiles

³/₄ cup sliced unpeeled cucumber

¹/₂ yellow onion, sliced

1 tablespoon plus 1¹/₂ teaspoons kosher salt

³/₄ cup cider vinegar

³/₄ cup sugar

2 cloves garlic

1¹/₂ teaspoons black peppercorns

1 teaspoon whole allspice

1 teaspoon cumin seeds

1 teaspoon coriander seeds

1 star anise pod

1 (³/₄-inch) piece cinnamon stick

2 bay leaves

1¹/₂ cups mayonnaise

Grated zest and juice of 1 lime

10 good-quality hot dogs

10 slices thin-cut bacon

3 small yellow onions, halved and thinly sliced

10 good-quality hot dog buns, split and toasted

Rice-o-licious

$^1/_4$ cup vegetable oil

$^3/_4$ cup diced yellow onion

2 teaspoons minced garlic

2 cups long-grain
white rice

$2^1/_3$ cups water

$1^2/_3$ cups canned
tomato puree

$2^1/_2$ teaspoons dried
Mexican oregano

1 teaspoon ground cumin

1 bay leaf

1 tablespoon kosher salt

$1^1/_2$ teaspoons freshly
ground black pepper

A boldly seasoned rice, laced with tomatoes, Mexican oregano, and cumin, this is the perfect accompaniment to most anything, including, of course, a dinner of tacos.

Preheat the oven to 350°F.

Heat the oil in a Dutch oven or other heavy pot with a lid over low heat. Add the onion and garlic and sauté for about 5 minutes, until translucent. Add the rice and continue to cook, stirring occasionally, for about 10 minutes, until the rice is lightly browned.

Add the water, tomato puree, oregano, cumin, bay leaf, salt, and pepper and simmer, uncovered, for 10 minutes. Cover, transfer the pot to the oven, and cook for 40 minutes, until the liquid is absorbed and the rice is tender.

Remove from the oven and let sit, covered, for 5 minutes. Uncover and let sit for 5 more minutes. Fluff with a fork and serve.

Rice-o-licious

Mama Virginia's chile
verde (page 129)

Frijoles borrachos
(page 93)

Classic guacamole
(page 53)

Pickled red onions
(page 41)

Not really refried beans

MAKES ABOUT 6 CUPS; SERVES 6

2¼ cups (1 pound) dried Vallarta, pinto, or black beans, picked over and rinsed

½ cup chopped yellow onion

2 cloves garlic, sliced

⅓ cup vegetable oil

4 teaspoons kosher salt

Three more ways to eat your beans

These beans are a great side, but they also make a delicious and healthy snack.

1. Warm up a tortilla and add a swipe of refried beans and a crumble of *queso fresco*.

2. Spice up the beans a bit more by adding some chile-infused salsa and you have a great party dip.

3. Use refried beans for the ultimate *torta* (page 64).

If the word *fry* conjures visions of an inevitable mess of oily splatter, take heart: these beans (which just happen to be vegan) are simmered until tender, pureed to the degree of chunkiness you like, and then flavored with garlic-and-onion-infused oil. It's a much neater way to go about making "refried" beans. At the restaurant, we use Rancho Gordo's extra-creamy and rich Vallarta beans. Order some for yourself (see page 94), or use more commonly available dried black beans or pinto beans.

In a large bowl, soak the beans in water to cover for at least 4 hours or up to overnight.

Add ¼ cup of the onion, 1 of the garlic cloves, and more water to cover if necessary and bring to a simmer over medium heat. Turn down the heat to medium-low, cover partially, and simmer for 1 to 1½ hours, until the beans are tender. The timing will depend on the age of the beans.

If the beans start to absorb all of the water and are not yet tender, add more water as necessary; there should always be at least 1¼ cups liquid when the beans are done.

Meanwhile, heat the oil in a small saucepan over medium-low heat and add the remaining ¼ cup chopped onion and 1 garlic clove. Cook, stirring, for about 4 minutes, until the onion and garlic are translucent and tender. Remove from the heat and set aside.

When the beans are ready, drain them, reserving the liquid. Transfer the beans, along with the onion and garlic with which they were cooked, to a large food processor (if you do not have a large processor, do this step in two batches). Add the reserved oil mixture, the salt, and ¾ cup of the reserved bean liquid and puree until the desired texture is achieved, smooth or slightly chunky as you like. This amount of liquid will yield a thick texture. If you prefer a looser texture, add more of the reserved liquid, but no but no more than 1¼ cups total.

To reheat, pour a little oil into a skillet over low heat and add the beans. Bring to temperature, stirring occasionally.

Frijoles borrachos

Spiked with tequila and beer, these pinto beans would be stumbling if they were people. To gild the lily, the recipe also has bacon. To balance that richness, we stir in some of our pickled vegetables (which can be replaced with canned pickled jalapeños and carrots). Serve these beans warm as the ultimate accompaniment to just about any taco. For an additional treat, garnish with a little crumbled *queso fresco*. If you're a vegetarian, feel free to omit the bacon. This recipe makes plenty, but it freezes well. *Pictured on page 91.*

In a large bowl, combine the beans with the water, adding more to cover if necessary. Let soak for at least 4 hours or up to overnight.

Place a large, heavy pot over medium-high heat. When the pot is hot, add the oil and then the bacon and cook, stirring occasionally, for about 5 minutes, until the bacon is crispy. Add the onions and cook, stirring occasionally, for about 5 minutes, until the onions begin to brown slightly at the edges. Add the pickled vegetables, beer, tequila, oregano, and the beans and their soaking water and bring almost to a boil. Turn down the heat to medium-low, cover partially, and simmer for 1 to 1½ hours, until the beans are tender. The timing will depend on the age of the beans.

Remove from the heat, add the salt, stir to mix, and then serve.

MAKES ABOUT 7 CUPS;
SERVES 8 TO 12

2¼ cups (about 1 pound) dried pinto beans, picked over and rinsed

7 cups water

1½ tablespoons vegetable oil

1 cup chopped bacon (about 5 ounces)

1¾ cups finely chopped yellow onion

⅓ cup finely chopped, drained Pickled cauliflower, carrots, and jalapeños (page 42)

1¼ cups dark Mexican beer

¼ cup tequila

1 tablespoon dried Mexican oregano, toasted in a dry skillet until fragrant

1½ tablespoons kosher salt

Steve Sando of Rancho Gordo:
The bean revolutionary

When Steve Sando started Rancho Gordo beans in 2003, no one had considered the plight of the humble bean, of which there are endless varieties in Mexico. "Early on, Thomas Keller whispered in my ear, 'You're doing something very important,'" says Sando of the famous French Laundry chef. And it was Sando's creamy and rich Vallarta bean, which had been on the verge of extinction, that was Keller's favorite. Although Keller's ringing endorsement helped get the word out about this extraordinary bean, Sando reports that the day Tacolicious started using the Vallarta for the restaurant's refried beans, the bean's "future was secured," because we use so much of it. (And yes, this is a not-so-humble brag.) Today Rancho Gordo grows around twenty thousand pounds of Vallarta beans annually. "The best way to save this stuff is to get people to eat it," Sando says.

"The best way to save this stuff is to get people to eat it," Sando says.

Although Rancho Gordo produces about 80 percent of its beans in California, the other 20 percent are commissioned and grown by independent, small farmers in Mexico for the company's XOXOC Project. "We grow twenty-five varieties and import about ten," says Sando. "And that's just like a cup out of the ocean."

From a nostalgic point of view, Sando's favorite bean might be the Rio Zape. "That was the first bean that got me hooked on the heirloom bean. It was so much better than your average pinto. Lately I've been eating a lot of Bull's Blood, which in Spanish is called Sangre de Toro. It makes a great pot likker (or bean broth, for those non-Southerners among you). And then there's the Rebosero, grown in Mexico by a woman named María. It's a great choice for refried beans, and even better if you make them vegetarian. And I'm a meat eater."

Steve Sando's tips for cooking beans

- Soak the beans in water to cover for 4 to 6 hours before cooking to help them retain their shape. If you forget to soak them, don't sweat it too much, however, especially if the beans are fresh (new crop).

- Avoid cooking beans in a pressure cooker. You won't get good bean broth using that method.

- Try cooking beans in a clay pot. Start by adding the aromatics, next bring the beans to a hard boil, and then reduce the heat as low as it will go.

- As for those embarrassing social situations that can occur when someone has had one bean too many? You just need to eat more beans more often, says Sando. "The more you eat beans, the more your body can digest them." Some believe that putting a sprig of epazote in a pot of beans—a traditional addition of Mexican cooks—will reduce that side effect, as well.

Cebollitas

At some of our favorite taco trucks, sweet, smoky *cebollitas*, along with pickled jalapeños, come with your order (generally served on a paper plate). While you could certainly chop up these grilled green onions and add them to a taco to great effect, they're more typically served as a little side treat to munch on.

12 green onions, root ends trimmed

1 tablespoon vegetable oil

Kosher salt

Prepare a hot fire for direct-heat cooking in a grill.

Rub the green onions with the oil and season with salt. Arrange the onions on the grill rack directly over the fire, placing them perpendicular to the bars so they don't fall through, and grill, turning them with tongs as needed to char evenly, for 2 to 3 minutes, until soft and lightly charred. Serve hot alongside your favorite tacos or grilled meats.

tacos,
tacos
+ tacos

99

When it comes to food, burgers are as synonymous with people's idea of American cuisine as tacos are with people's perception of the Mexican table. Today, the taco, like the burger, has become an international icon—a handheld comfort food that has been embraced worldwide.

It hasn't always been this way. Although the citizens of Mexico have been romancing tasty morsels of food folded up in corn tortillas for more than a millennium, the taco, as we think of it today, only came into its own in the twentieth century. A hundred years later, there are versions of tacos everywhere from Sweden, where a popular chain called Taco Bar dishes out Americanized hard-shell tacos, to the United States, where inspired "taco" culture clashes, such as the Korean short rib variety served up at Los Angeles's now-famous Koji BBQ truck, have taken hold.

In the United States, pretty much all of the border states—from Texas to New Mexico—have long served as entry points for Mexican food. California is no different. In San Francisco, where we live, tacos exist on a subconscious level. The heady aroma of corn tortillas mixing with chiles and braised meats and vegetables is part of our daily craving. At home, we wake up to a breakfast of scrambled eggs in tortillas, topped with a shake of Tapatío. Out on the town, we

pop into a taqueria for a snack. At our favorite trucks, we wolf down street food–size *carne asada* tacos from grease-laden paper plates. We even choose to have tacos catered at special occasions (Tacolicious has been asked to cater everything from weddings to bar mitzvahs).

The only limitation to the pleasures of a good taco is feeling bound to some nebulous idea of tradition. Jeffrey M. Pilcher, author of *Planet Taco: A Global History of Mexican Food*, eloquently sums up the limitations of authenticity: "Iconic recipes exist only on the page of cookbooks; in practice, they are adapted constantly to suit available ingredients. . . . One woman's secret ingredient ruins the entire dish for another."

Although the following recipes are almost all based on classic Mexican cuisine, at Tacolicious we also have no problem throwing tradition to the wind on occasion, incorporating a little *je ne sais quoi* when the time calls for it. So go forth into your kitchen armed with this book, but once you get the hang of it, feel liberated to adapt the recipes to suit your own taste or available pantry items. Add a dash of chopped tarragon, if you feel like it, or try a new vegetable combo, like butternut squash and radicchio. Serve tacos prepped to order or plunk a big pot of braised meat and a stack of tortillas on the table.

Guajillo-braised beef short rib taco

**MAKES 16 TACOS;
SERVES 4 TO 6**

8 guajillo chiles, stemmed
and seeded

3 dried chipotle chiles,
stemmed and seeded

2 to 4 tablespoons
vegetable oil

3 pounds boneless beef
short ribs

1 large yellow onion,
coarsely chopped

2 cloves garlic, coarsely
chopped

1 (12-ounce) bottle Negro
Modelo or other dark
Mexican beer

2 teaspoons ground cumin

1 teaspoon freshly ground
black pepper

1¹/₂ tablespoons dried
Mexican oregano

1¹/₂ tablespoons
kosher salt

¹/₂ cup water

Corn tortillas, warmed
(see page 108), for serving

Chopped white onion,
chopped fresh cilantro,
salsa of choice, and lime
wedges, for serving

Everyone has his or her favorite Tacolicious taco, but this is mine, hands down. These short ribs cooked slowly with guajillos break down into the perfect braised meat: rich, a tad spicy, and appropriately messy—a true sign of greatness. You can ask your butcher to bone the ribs for you, or you can just cook them with the bone in and then bone them before shredding the meat. You'll need 5 pounds of bone-in short ribs to yield the required 3 pounds of meat. This dish can be on the spicy side, so if you're really sensitive to heat, cut back a little on the chiles.

Preheat the oven to 325°F.

Working in two batches if necessary to avoid crowding, lightly toast all of the chiles in a dry, heavy skillet over medium heat for 30 seconds on each side, until fragrant but not blackened. Set them aside on a plate.

Heat 2 tablespoons of the oil in a Dutch oven or other heavy pot with a lid over medium-high heat. When the oil is hot, working in batches to avoid crowding, add the meat and sear for about 3 minutes on each side, until the pieces have formed a uniformly browned crust. Add more oil to the pot as needed to prevent scorching. As the pieces are ready, set them aside on a plate.

Add the onion to the same same pot over medium heat and cook, stirring occasionally, for about 5 minutes, until it starts to brown. Add the garlic and cook for an additional 2 minutes.

Pour in the beer, add the toasted chiles, and turn down the heat to low. Simmer uncovered, stirring occasionally, for about 5 minutes, until the chiles have softened and are pliable. Remove from the heat and let cool.

Transfer the contents of the pot to a blender and reserve the pot. Add the cumin, pepper, oregano, salt, and water to the blender and blend the mixture on high speed until smooth and the consistency of cream, adding more water if needed to thin the mixture a bit.

Return the seared meat to the pot and pour in the chile mixture. Cover, transfer to the oven, and cook, stirring occasionally, for 3 to 4 hours, until the meat is fork-tender.

Remove from the oven and, using tongs or a couple of forks, shred the meat in the pot. Taste and adjust the seasoning with salt if needed. Serve with the tortillas, onion, cilantro, salsa, and lime.

Telmo's taco de lengua

**MAKES ABOUT 16 TACOS;
SERVES 4 TO 6**

1 beef tongue, about
3 pounds, rinsed

1 large yellow onion,
coarsely chopped

2 large carrots, peeled and
coarsely chopped

2 celery stalks,
coarsely chopped

10 cloves garlic

1 jalapeño chile, stemmed
and halved lengthwise

1 bunch oregano
(about 1 cup)

4 bay leaves

2 teaspoons black
peppercorns

1 teaspoon whole allspice

2 star anise pods

1/4 cup kosher salt

4 tablespoons
vegetable oil

Corn tortillas, warmed
(see page 108), for serving

Chopped white onion,
chopped fresh cilantro,
salsa of choice, and lime
wedges, for serving

Let go of the opinion that tongue is only for the adventurous diner. Fans of *lengua* are diehards—and for good reason. The meltingly tender meat, poached at first and then crisped up at the very end, tastes like one of the best beef tacos you've ever had. With risks come rewards.

In a large pot, combine the tongue, onion, carrots, celery, garlic, chile, oregano, bay leaves, peppercorns, allspice, star anise, and salt with water to cover by 2 inches. Place over medium-high heat and bring to a boil. Turn down the heat to medium and cook, uncovered, at a rolling simmer for 2 to 2 1/2 hours, until the tongue is easily pierced through with a knife. As the tongue cooks, it will float to the surface. Add more water as needed to cover. If necessary, turn the tongue over a few times as it simmers to ensure it cooks evenly.

Remove the tongue from the liquid and let cool to room temperature. Discard the cooking liquid. Using a paring knife, peel off the skin of the tongue and cut away any fat and gristle. Cut the meat into 1/2-inch cubes.

Heat 2 tablespoons of the oil in a large, heavy sauté pan or skillet over medium-high heat. When the oil is hot, put half of the tongue in the pan and cook, stirring or tossing occasionally, for 5 to 6 minutes, until the cubes are browned and crisped on all sides. Transfer to a bowl and repeat with the remaining oil and tongue.

Serve with the tortillas, onion, cilantro, salsa, and lime.

Nose-to-tail tacos

Propelled by the nose-to-tail butchery movement, the consumption of offal—or innards, as some know it—has been on the rise among a certain dining cognoscenti. Still, for many chicken-breast-centric Americans who didn't grow up on things like tongue, feasting on these parts of the animal can take some getting used to, no matter how good one's intentions. It's illuminating to travel to a country where eating the whole animal isn't a political statement—it's just dinner. In Mexico, park yourself at any street stall and you'll watch people of all sorts—men and women—casually order up tacos made of, say, brain, which is matter-of-factly pulled out of a boiling cauldron of meats, chopped up, and served forward.

Potato and homemade chorizo taco

Called *papas con chorizo* in Spanish—a much more fun way to say it—this classic combo is easy to put together with a quick recipe for chorizo. Although making your own sausage sounds impressive, actually doing it is no sweat (unless you spice it up with extra chiles, which you certainly could do).

To make the chorizo, place the chiles and sauce, vinegar, garlic, paprika, oregano, coriander, and salt in a blender. Puree until a smooth paste forms, stopping to scrape down the sides as needed.

Put the pork in a large bowl, add the chile paste, and, using your hands, mix to coat the meat evenly. Set aside.

Line a plate with paper towels. Heat the oil in a skillet, preferably cast iron, over medium heat. Add the potato cubes and cook, tossing them occasionally, for about 8 minutes, until they are golden brown and cooked through. Salt lightly, then, using a slotted spoon, transfer to the lined plate.

Heat a large sauté pan over medium-high heat. When the pan is hot, add the chorizo and cook, breaking up the meat with a wooden spoon, for about 12 minutes, until cooked through. Add the potatoes and toss and stir for 1 to 2 minutes longer, until evenly mixed and heated through.

Serve with the tortillas, onion, cilantro, salsa, and lime.

MAKES ABOUT 16 TACOS;
SERVES 4 TO 6

Chorizo

1/4 cup chopped chipotle chiles in adobo sauce (a mix of chiles and sauce)

3 tablespoons cider vinegar

5 cloves garlic, coarsely chopped

2 tablespoons sweet paprika

1 tablespoon dried Mexican oregano

1 tablespoon ground coriander

1 tablespoon kosher salt

1 3/4 pounds ground pork

3 tablespoons vegetable oil

1 large russet potato, peeled and cut into 1/4-inch cubes

Kosher salt

Corn tortillas, warmed (see page 108), for serving

Chopped white onion, chopped fresh cilantro, salsa of choice, and lime wedges, for serving

Just add eggs

There's hardly a taco filling in this book that wouldn't benefit from the addition of eggs—scrambled, fried, or poached. This chorizo-and-potato recipe is a natural, of course. Simply whisk together a few eggs in a bowl, and when the chorizo and potatoes are sizzling in the pan over medium heat, pour in the eggs and scramble everything up (chopped green onions would be another great addition). Eat as a taco or not. The Spring booty filling (page 133) would benefit from this scrambled egg treatment, too. Or lightly panfry a tortilla, place it on a plate, top it with warmed *carnitas* (page 124) and a few avocado slices, and then slide on a fried egg and finish with a dash of hot sauce or salsa. You can also take a braised meat, such as a soupy pot of *chile verde* (page 129), ladle it into a bowl, top it with a poached egg, and serve it with tortillas on the side.

Everything you need to know about corn tortillas

In Mexico, corn tortillas are the true star of the country's cuisine, with flour tortillas playing a supporting role. What's more, corn tortillas are wonderfully versatile throughout their life span. The freshest, most pliable ones, made of only corn and the slaked lime in which the corn is soaked, are used for tacos or served warm as an accompaniment to a meal, just as you would offer bread. Slightly less fresh ones are rolled up into enchiladas; day-old tortillas are often fried and used for dishes like *chilaquiles*. And this is just the beginning. In Mexico, the list of things you can make with tortillas is nearly endless.

Tortillas are best made fresh

Sure, it's lovely to imagine that Mexico is full of *abuelitas* patting out tortillas by hand. And yes, we've visited small villages like Tekit in Yucatán, where the mother of one of our cooks, using a press to shape them and a wood-fired *comal* to cook them, makes a bucket's worth of tortillas every morning. But I'd say she's the exception to the rule.

Most people in Mexico buy their fresh tortillas from a place with a machine that forms the *masa* into rounds and then sends them on their merry way on a conveyor belt to cook over a hot flame before they land in the hands of a worker. Even Mexican supermarkets have these machines. And if tortillas are not made on-site, they're bought nearby and resold that day. If you see condensation in the plastic bag of tortillas, you can pretty much assume they're fresh.

Although you may not have great tortilla access where you live, we can help you make the most of what's available.

> In Mexico, the list of things you can make with tortillas is nearly endless.

Thoughts on homemade tortillas

At Tacolicious, we use tortillas made for us by our favorite local *tortilleria*. We go through so many, we couldn't possibly make ours by hand. But even at home, we prefer good quality *tortilleria* tortillas; their slightly chewy texture holds up to the braised meats we love so. This is not to say that making corn tortillas by hand isn't rewarding (not to mention delicious). Just make sure to use good-quality *masa*.

Choosing the best prepackaged tortillas

Although we recommend that you use the freshest tortillas you can find, we accept the fact that most people buy tortillas at supermarkets because of convenience. Today, tortillas made with a mixture of wheat and corn have become popular, so read the fine print. They are often softer and more flexible than pure-corn tortillas, but they also taste and cook differently, burning more quickly than their pure counterparts. (They are not gluten free, either, if that is a concern.) If you're concerned about additives, it's good to know that traditional tortillas are made from corn that has been treated with slaked lime and contain nothing more. The only downside to this kind of purity is that the shelf life is shorter.

We did a taste test, cooking up a dozen brands of corn tortillas from Safeway, Trader Joe's, and Whole Foods. The biggest takeaway? Not all tortillas are created equal. Not even a little bit. Surprisingly, the store brand from one of the country's most revered supermarkets was the worst that we tasted, unless you have a penchant for eating cardboard. Our top three are listed on the facing page, but if these aren't available, conduct your own taste test to find a good brand.

The ideal size for a taco

In Mexico and in traditional Mexican markets in the United States, you'll see tortillas in all sizes. On the streets (this includes carts and trucks), tacos are usually made with tortillas about 4½ inches in diameter, just right for an on-the-run, two- to three-bite snack. Whatever you choose, avoid tortillas that are too big. The best taco-eating experience should leave you wanting a little more.

Storing tortillas

Tortillas are best eaten fresh. However, to extend their life beyond a couple of days, tortillas should be stored in a closed plastic bag in the refrigerator. Use your nose to determine when the *masa* smells too sour to use, and remember that tortillas without any preservatives dry out and become stiff quickly.

How to heat up a tortilla: the pious way and the (ever-so-slightly) sinful way

Although tortillas are technically already cooked, they need to be toasted in order to show off their best self. Traditionally, a tortilla is heated up on a griddlelike pan, or *comal* (a heavy, dry cast-iron skillet is a good substitute), for about 15 seconds on each side, until it puffs a bit and starts to smell corny. We are completely in support of this.

However, at Tacolicious, we add a little oil to the cooking surface, something that we learned from San Francisco's beloved La Taqueria. It might be just

Avoid tortillas that are too big. The best taco-eating experience should leave you wanting a little more.

a teaspoon less pious than the above technique, but trust us, it has delicious results.

To heat your tortillas with oil, drizzle a thin slick of vegetable oil onto a heavy skillet placed over medium heat. When the oil is hot, heat the tortilla on it for about 15 seconds, until the tortilla turns a bit more golden. When the aroma of heaven hits your nose, drizzle a tiny bit of oil on the top of the tortilla, flip it over, and heat for 15 seconds longer. The idea is not to fry it but to bring out more of its corny self.

Our tacos are each wrapped in two tortillas, so we stack them: once the bottom tortilla has cooked, drizzle oil on the top tortilla, and flip the paired tortillas over just as you would a single tortilla. The middle of the two tortillas will meld together slightly in the process. Leave them that way. It helps make for a nice sturdy taco.

How to keep a stack of tortillas warm

Tacos make a party, but standing at the stove heating tortilla after tortilla to order for your guests is more than a bit arduous. We've seen suggestions for microwaving a stack of tortillas, but as tempting as it may sound, we can't recommend it. It leaves you with steamy, flaccid, flavorless tortillas.

Instead, to keep a stack of tortillas warm, heat them one by one as you normally would, stacking them as you go on in a clean kitchen towel and keeping them covered with the towel. Once you have enough, tightly wrap the towel-covered tortillas in aluminum foil and place in a 200°F oven for up to an hour.

Our top three supermarket tortillas

Trader Joe's

"Made from freshly ground corn" is what it says on the label of these pleasant, almost rustic-tasting tortillas, made the old-fashioned way with no preservatives.

Mi Rancho Hand-Crafted Organic

Sold in a tinted yellow bag that makes them look misleadingly sunny, these tortillas are still quite good, especially considering that they're certified organic and made with non-GMO corn. Guar gum is an ingredient, but there are worse things out there.

Guerrero

Telmo calls this commonly found (at least on the West Coast) brand the "Honda Civic" of tortillas, meaning that the tortillas have a reliably good flavor and texture, though they also have quite a few additives.

Three-chile bistec adobado taco with cebollitas

MAKES ABOUT 16 TACOS;
SERVES 4 TO 6

2 ancho chiles, stemmed and seeded

2 guajillo chiles, stemmed and seeded

1 cascabel chile, stemmed and seeded

$1/3$ cup cider vinegar

$1/3$ cup hot water

3 tablespoons vegetable oil

$1/4$ yellow onion, chopped

4 cloves garlic, chopped

1 teaspoon ground cumin

1 tablespoon kosher salt

1 teaspoon freshly ground black pepper

3 pounds flank steak, cut into 6 equal pieces (to make it easier to grill)

Cebollitas (page 96)

Corn tortillas, warmed (see page 108), for serving

Chopped white onion, chopped fresh cilantro, salsa of choice, and lime wedges, for serving

Adobado is a traditional preparation in which meat is marinated with chiles, vinegar, and seasonings, though there's no hard-and-fast rule about what you must include. This classic grilled steak recipe is best made with a beef cut that has some chew. We like flank, but skirt steak or tri-tip is equally good. Serve sliced or chopped on a platter with a tangle of sweet, grilled *cebollitas* and a pile of warm tortillas. If you can't find a cascabel chile, add another guajillo. A good salsa, such as The legendary orange sauce (page 35), is key.

Combine the ancho, guajillo, and cascabel chiles in a bowl with the vinegar and hot water, top the chiles with a weight to keep them submerged, and let stand for about 15 minutes, until softened.

Meanwhile, heat the oil in a sauté pan over medium heat. Add the onion and garlic and sauté for about 15 minutes, until browned. Remove from the heat and let cool.

When the chiles have softened, transfer them and their soaking liquid to a blender. Add the cooled onion and garlic and their oil and the cumin, salt, and pepper and blend on high speed until a thick paste forms. Pour the paste into a bowl and cover.

Put the flank steak in a heavy-duty zip-top plastic bag, add the chile paste, and seal the bag closed. Massage the contents of the bag to coat both sides of each piece of meat evenly with the paste. Alternatively, place the steak pieces and the chile paste in a shallow baking dish, turn the pieces to coat evenly, and cover with plastic wrap. Marinate in the refrigerator for at least 2 hours or up to 12 hours (the longer the better).

Prepare a medium-hot fire for direct-heat cooking in a grill. Remove the steak from the marinade and let it come to room temperature.

Arrange the steak on the grill rack directly over the fire and grill, turning once, for 4 to 5 minutes on each side for medium-rare. Transfer to a cutting board and let rest for a few minutes. While the steak is resting, grill the *cebollitas*.

Chop the steak into bite-size pieces and season with salt and pepper. Serve with the tortillas, onion, cilantro, salsa, and lime. Serve the grilled onions on the side for munching or chop them coarsely to add to the tacos.

Old-school taco

Hot Sauce

1/4 cup ketchup

1/4 cup white wine vinegar

1 tablespoon Worcestershire sauce

2 tablespoons unsulfured molasses

2 tablespoons sauce from chipotle chiles in adobo sauce

1 tablespoon Tapatío or similar Mexican hot sauce

3/4 teaspoon ground cumin

3/4 teaspoon sweet paprika

3/4 teaspoon onion powder

3/4 teaspoon garlic powder

1 teaspoon kosher salt

1/4 teaspoon freshly ground black pepper

Filling

4 tablespoons vegetable oil

1 1/2 pounds ground beef

3/4 cup finely chopped yellow onion

1 1/2 tablespoons finely chopped garlic

2 tablespoons chili powder

2 teaspoons ground cumin

2 teaspoons onion powder

2 teaspoons garlic powder

2 teaspoons kosher salt

You can call these Americanized tacos inspired by the Ortega taco kit sacrilege, but you must also admit that they taste great. At the restaurant, we serve these on Tuesdays only. For this, we fry up our own hard-shell tacos, but for home cooking, save yourself a lot of trouble and just buy them (Old El Paso brand is our recommendation). Please don't try to get too gourmet with this recipe. Stay patriotic and serve these tacos as they're meant to be: topped with grated orange Cheddar cheese.

To make the hot sauce, in a blender, combine all of the ingredients and puree until smooth. Taste and adjust the seasoning with salt if needed. Set aside until ready to serve.

To make the filling, heat 2 tablespoons of the oil in a large sauté pan over high heat. When the oil is hot, add the beef and cook, breaking up the meat with a wooden spoon, for about 5 minutes, until browned. (If this is too much beef for your pan to accommodate comfortably, cook it in two batches.) Using a slotted spoon, transfer the beef to a bowl and set aside. Discard the fat in the pan.

Return the pan to medium-high heat and add the remaining 2 tablespoons oil. Add the onion and garlic and sauté for about 2 minutes, scraping up and incorporating any bits of browned beef stuck to the pan bottom. Add the chili powder, cumin, onion powder, garlic powder, salt, and black pepper and cook, stirring, for about 1 minute longer. Return the beef to the pan and sauté for several minutes to bring the flavors together. Stir in the adobo sauce. Keep warm until ready to serve.

To serve, put the cheese, lettuce, and tomatoes in separate bowls and place on the table. Crisp the taco shells in the oven according to the package directions. Place the taco shells, the warm beef, and the hot sauce on the table alongside the condiments and invite diners to make their own tacos.

The history of the hard shell

Though the true inventor of the first Mexican-American hard shell taco is disputed, Glen Bell definitely made the most money from it. In 1951, Bell started selling hard-shell tacos for nineteen cents apiece at his drive-in hamburger stand in San Bernardino, California (not far, actually, from some other guys who had another burger stand—one that went by the name of McDonald's). In 1962, after tinkering with a few other taco concepts, he launched Taco Bell. In 2010, at the age of 86, Bell passed away, leaving a legacy of 5,600 Taco Bells around the world. Two years later, Taco Bell introduced the Doritos Locos Taco, which features shell flavors such as Cool Ranch and Nacho Cheese. Love it or run screaming from it, it is reported to have racked up more than one billion dollars in sales.

1 teaspoon freshly ground black pepper

1/4 cup sauce from chipotle chiles in adobo sauce

1 1/2 cups shredded Cheddar cheese

2 cups finely chopped romaine lettuce

1 cup diced Roma tomatoes (about 3 small tomatoes)

8 to 12 store-bought taco shells

Birria de chivo taco

1 tablespoon vegetable oil

4 guajillo chiles

4 ancho chiles

2 Roma tomatoes

4 large cloves garlic

2 cups hot water

2 tablespoons
cider vinegar

3 tablespoons kosher salt

1 teaspoon freshly ground
black pepper

1 teaspoon ground cumin

1 teaspoon ground
coriander

1/2 teaspoon ground
allspice

1/4 teaspoon ground cloves

1/4 teaspoon ground
cinnamon

5 pounds bone-in goat
shoulder (ask your butcher
to cut it into 3-inch pieces)

3 cups boiling water,
or as needed

Corn tortillas, warmed (see
page 108), for serving

Chopped white onion,
chopped fresh cilantro,
salsa of choice, and lime
wedges, for serving

Birria, a hearty, warming stew, or *guisado* (see page 116), is typically made with goat meat (*chivo*), though it is also made with lamb, which can be substituted here. It is a delicious filling for tacos but is more traditionally served with tortillas on the side, which are used for dipping into the broth. There are different methods for making *birria*: One calls for braising the meat as you would for any stew. This one directs you to steam the meat in the oven and then mix it with the marinade and return it to the oven to finish. When Telmo and Joe were in Guadalajara, they ate *birria* cooked in banana leaves, which add a nice herbal element. To do this, all you have to do is wrap the goat in the banana leaves before putting it in the steamer.

Before you say "no way" to eating goat meat, we suggest you give it a good college try. Not only is it delicious, but it is also leaner and milder than you might think, and a sustainable choice to boot. The tacos are accompanied here with onion, cilantro, and lime, but they would also be good with cabbage, radishes, and *crema*.

Heat the oil in a heavy skillet over medium-high heat. When the oil is hot, add the guajillo chiles and fry, turning them with tongs, for about 45 seconds on each side, until fragrant. Be careful not to let them burn. Transfer to a plate and let cool. Repeat the process with the ancho chiles and add them to the plate.

Turn down the heat to medium and add the whole tomatoes and garlic cloves. Turn the tomatoes until the skin has blistered on all sides. Turn the garlic until it is caramelized. Both should be ready in 8 to 10 minutes. Transfer the tomatoes and garlic to a plate and let cool, then peel the cooled tomatoes.

Using a knife or scissors, remove the stems from the chiles, then slit each chile lengthwise and shake out all the seeds. Place the chiles in a bowl, add the hot water, top the chiles with a weight to keep them submerged, and let stand for about 10 minutes, until softened.

Put the chiles and 1 cup of their soaking water and the tomatoes and garlic in a blender. Add the vinegar, salt, pepper, cumin, coriander, allspice, cloves, and cinnamon and puree until a smooth paste forms. You should have about 2 1/2 cups.

Put the goat meat in a large, heavy-duty zip-top plastic bag, add 1 1/2 cups of the chile paste, and seal the bag closed. Massage the contents of the bag to coat the meat evenly with the paste. Alternatively, place the goat meat and 1 1/2 cups of the chile paste in a large, shallow baking dish, turn the meat to coat evenly, and cover with plastic wrap. Reserve the remaining chile paste for use later. Marinate the goat in the refrigerator for at least 4 hours or up to 24 hours.

To cook the *birria*, preheat the oven to 350°F. Place a steamer basket in a Dutch oven or other large, heavy pot with a lid. Add the boiling water to the pot. The water should reach just below the bottom of the basket; add more if necessary. Transfer the goat meat to the basket and top with any marinade remaining in the bag or dish. Cover the pot with heavy-duty aluminum foil and then with the lid.

Transfer the pot to the oven and cook for 3 to 4 hours, until the meat is fork-tender. Check the water level after 1 1/2 to 2 hours and add more boiling water if the level has dropped.

Remove the pot from the oven (leave the oven set at 350°F), uncover, and remove the meat from the steamer basket. Pull the meat from the bones, discard the bones, and shred the meat with a couple of forks. Remove the steamer basket from the pot, leaving the brothy water behind. Place the meat back into the broth, and toss with a gradual amount of the chile paste until the flavor suits your preference (it can get too salty if you're not careful).

Place the uncovered pot of goat back into the oven and cook for 30 minutes longer.

Remove from the oven, transfer the meat to a bowl, and add enough leftover juice from the pot to moisten the meat to your taste. If you will use the meat for tacos, you won't want it too soupy. If you are serving the meat as a stew with the tortillas on the side, you may want it to be soupier.

Serve the goat with the tortillas, onion, cilantro, salsa, and lime wedges.

Where to get your goat?

Although you can generally find goat meat at Mexican or halal butcher shops, you can also order high-quality goat meat from Preferred Meats (visit their website at preferredmeats.com), which was started by famed livestock rancher Bill Niman. Another resource is Copeland Family Farms (goatmeats .com), where goat is called by its French name, *chevon*.

Taco de guisado: The king of tacos

When many people in the United States think of tacos, they immediately think of classic fillings like carne asada (grilled steak) or the familiar carnitas (braised, then crisped pork). But in Mexico, taco stands that cater specifically to lovers of long-cooked meats and vegetables abound. These spots specialize in tacos de guisado, which are essentially tacos with stewed meat.

Guisados *rule on the taco spectrum. There's something about a warm corn tortilla soaking up braised meat that can't be beat. The experience is downright lusty, as the inevitable and delicious mess of juices runs down your wrist and drips onto your plate. Add little bits of chopped onion and pickled chile to the mix, and the juxtaposition of soft and braisey and crunchy and spicy is addictive.*

When you're in Mexico, you'll know a guisado place when you see it. At famous spots like Tacos Hola in Mexico City's Condesa neighborhood, rows of cazuelas (clay pots) filled with myriad braised concoctions are visible so patrons can choose what they want. You'll find everything from cochinita pibil and picadillo to chicharrónes cooked in salsa to vegetables such as cactus and greens.

For the home cook, guisados are eminently practical. They can simmer on the stove top or in the oven for hours, and they can be packed up, frozen, and reheated with no problem. In fact, because of these user-friendly qualities, tacos de guisado were all we served when Tacolicious started out as a little stand at the farmers' market. In this book we share some favorites: Birria de chiva (page 114), Lamb adobo (page 118), Cochinita pibil (page 126), Mama Virginia's chile verde (page 129), and Shot-and-a-beer braised chicken (page 132).

> Guisados rule on the taco spectrum. There's something about a warm corn tortilla soaking up braised meat that can't be beat.

Guajillo-braised beef
short ribs (page 102)

Lamb adobo taco with spices and orange

If you are a dinner guest in our house, it's very likely that Joe and I will serve you lamb. We both love its big flavor, which is one reason that this recipe, inspired by a dish served at the Elote Cafe in Sedona, Arizona, is a favorite. Full of spices like cinnamon, cumin, and cloves, it's what you want on a cold night. Serve it as a taco, of course, but we enjoy it even more as a stew, served on the shank, with warm tortillas alongside. The sauce itself is so bold and flavorful that we don't think you need to put out a salsa. A little dish of Pickled red onions (page 41) is a nice addition, however.

MAKES ABOUT 12 TACOS;
SERVES 4 TO 6

Sauce

6 large cloves garlic, unpeeled

6 ancho chiles, stemmed and seeded

4 cups freshly squeezed orange juice

2 tablespoons dark brown sugar

2 tablespoons dried Mexican oregano

2 tablespoons cider vinegar

2 teaspoons kosher salt

2 teaspoons freshly ground black pepper

2 teaspoons ground cumin

$1/8$ teaspoon ground cloves

1 (3-inch) stick canela (Mexican cinnamon) or regular cinnamon

2 bay leaves

To make the sauce, toast the garlic on a dry, heavy skillet over medium heat, turning occasionally, for about 12 minutes, until softened and speckled brown. Transfer to a small plate to cool. Add the chiles to the same pan and toast, turning once, for about 30 seconds on each side, until fragrant but not blackened. Take care that they do not burn.

Pour the orange juice into a saucepan, then add the sugar, oregano, vinegar, salt, pepper, cumin, cloves, cinnamon, and bay leaves and stir to mix. Peel the garlic cloves and add them to the pan. Cover, bring to a boil, turn down the heat to a simmer, and cook for about 10 minutes, until the chiles have softened.

Remove the cinnamon stick and bay leaves and reserve. Let the sauce cool slightly, then transfer to a blender and puree until very smooth.

Preheat the oven to 325°F.

Sprinkle the lamb shanks evenly with the salt and pepper. Heat the oil in a Dutch oven or other large, heavy ovenproof pot with a lid over medium-high heat. Add 2 of the shanks and sear, turning them as needed to color evenly, for 7 to 8 minutes, until golden brown. Transfer to a plate and repeat with the remaining 2 shanks.

Add the pureed sauce and the reserved cinnamon and bay leaves to the pot and bring to a boil over high heat, stirring constantly. Add the shanks. If needed, pour in hot water so the liquid reaches halfway up the sides of the shanks. Cover, transfer to the oven, and cook, turning the shanks every 45 minutes or so to ensure they are evenly exposed to the sauce, for about 2 hours, until the meat is very tender when pierced with a fork.

Transfer the shanks to a platter and cover with aluminum foil. Skim off and discard the fat from the surface of the sauce. Place the pot over medium-high heat, bring to a boil, and boil the sauce for about 10 minutes, until thick enough to coat the meat.

Uncover the shanks. If making tacos, remove the meat from the bones and shred it with a couple of forks. Put the meat in a serving bowl, mix with enough of the sauce to make it nice and juicy, and serve with the tortillas, onion, cilantro, and lime. Or serve the shanks with a good amount of sauce spooned over the top and pass the tortillas, onion, cilantro, and lime wedges at the table.

4 lamb shanks, about
1 pound each

1 teaspoon kosher salt

1 teaspoon freshly ground
black pepper

2 tablespoons
vegetable oil

12 corn tortillas, warmed
(see page 108), for serving

Chopped white onion,
chopped fresh cilantro,
and lime wedges,
for serving

Tacos al pastor: authentic or not?

The truth about "cuisine" is that it's a shape-shifter, and thank goodness for that. What might be considered a classic today was probably considered an abomination at some point. *Tacos al pastor* are a great example. The technique of layering meat on a vertical spit and cooking it by a charcoal fire was reportedly brought to Puebla, Mexico, in the 1930s by Lebanese immigrants, who prefer lamb to pork (and put it all in pita bread and call it *shawarma*). About thirty years later, this brilliant method of cooking made its way to Mexico City, and *taqueros* started selling what is now the runaway hit called *tacos al pastor*. Today in DF, different vendors claim to be the original inventor—but really, who cares? What matters is that it's delicious.

Off-the-spit pork al pastor taco

Walk into Mosto, and the first thing that greets you is the fragrant aroma of our *al pastor* spit, or *trompo* as it's called in Mexico. From it, a cook carves off slices of achiote-stained pork, places them on a warm tortilla, and tops the meat with a few chunks of sweet-tart pineapple (which, in the hands of a showman, is skillfully sliced and lobbed off directly into the taco). This recipe, however, is adapted for home cooking. The meat is given that critical bit of smoky char by grilling it. (Although we don't grill the pineapple here before dicing it, it's a nice touch if you don't mind an extra step.) Look for pork butt sold presliced at Latin butcher shops, ask your butcher to slice it for you, or freeze the pork for about an hour, until it is firm enough to slice, and then slice it yourself.

Put the chiles in a bowl, add hot water to cover, top the chiles with a weight to keep them submerged, and let soak for about 15 minutes, until softened.

Drain the chiles and transfer them to a blender. Add the garlic, onion, pineapple juice, lime juice, vinegar, achiote paste, salt, oregano, and cumin and puree until smooth.

Put the pork in a large, heavy-duty zip-top plastic bag, add the chile puree, and seal the bag closed. Massage the contents of the bag to coat the pork evenly with the puree. Alternatively, place the pork slices and puree in a shallow baking dish, turn the slices to coat evenly, and cover with plastic wrap. Marinate in the refrigerator for at least 8 hours or up to 24 hours.

Prepare a medium-hot fire for direct-heat cooking in a grill. Remove the pork from the marinade and let come to room temperature.

Arrange the pork on the grill rack directly over the fire and grill, turning once with tongs, for about 3 minutes on each side, until it has a bit of char and is cooked through but not dry. Transfer the pork to a cutting board, chop into 1/2-inch cubes, and place in a serving bowl.

Serve with the tortillas, pineapple, onion, cilantro, salsa, and lime.

MAKES ABOUT 16 TACOS;
SERVES 4 TO 6

4 guajillo chiles, stemmed and seeded

5 cloves garlic, coarsely chopped

1/2 yellow onion, coarsely chopped

1 cup unsweetened pineapple juice

1/3 cup freshly squeezed lime juice

1/4 cup cider vinegar

2 tablespoons achiote paste

2 tablespoons kosher salt

1 tablespoon dried Mexican oregano

1 teaspoon ground cumin

3 1/2 pounds boneless pork shoulder, cut into 1/2-inch-thick slices (reserve any trimmings for another use)

Corn tortillas, warmed (see page 108), for serving

1 cup diced fresh pineapple, at room temperature

Chopped white onion, chopped fresh cilantro, salsa of choice, and lime wedges, for serving

La Palma:
The tortilleria that could

Since the summer of 2009, when Tacolicious was nothing but a weekly stand at the Ferry Plaza farmers' market, our tortilla needs have grown by leaps and bounds. We couldn't keep up with making our own tortillas if we wanted to. Luckily, La Palma, the tenacious, sixty-one-year-old, family-run tortilleria and Mexicatessen located in the Mission District, has continued to come through for Tacolicious, cooking up chewy, fresh tortillas better than we could ever make them ourselves. Out of their not-so-large storefront on Twenty-Fourth Street, they make more than eight million tortillas annually for our four restaurants.

Although some tortillerias buy their masa elsewhere, La Palma makes its tortillas starting with the soaking and then cooking of the corn (overcook it and you're going to have a dry tortilla). Theresa Pasion—or Terry as we call her—their general manager, claims that San Francisco's climate is perfect for making masa. "It's not too hot here. Corn is temperamental, and in warm weather, it can go sour in like twenty minutes."

The bittersweet truth about fresh tortillas is that they have a very short shelf life—at the very most, forty-eight hours—before they start to become dry and brittle. That's why the best thing you can do is buy your tortillas daily. But even Terry admits that things are different in the United States, where "we're buying for the week because we're working our butts off. Whereas in Mexico, you buy your tortillas for the day—or maybe even for the morning for breakfast and go back in the afternoon."

When it comes to heating up tortillas, Terry is a purist. She doesn't like them cooked with a tiny bit of oil like we do at Tacolicious. Not a woman to mince words, she says flatly, "I'm totally against that." But her exactitude is what keeps our tortillas perfect. "I get really crazy if they have marks on them or are too rough," she says. "I'm always saying that I want the tortillas as nice and soft as a baby's butt! And the guys that I work with are like, 'Here she goes again!'"

Carnitas taco

MAKES ABOUT 16 TACOS;
SERVES 4 TO 6

2¹⁄₂ pounds boneless pork shoulder, cut into 2- to 3-inch cubes

1 cup sliced yellow onion

3 cloves garlic, crushed

3 tablespoons dark brown sugar

1¹⁄₂ tablespoons kosher salt

1¹⁄₂ teaspoons dried Mexican oregano

1 bay leaf

2 tablespoons freshly squeezed orange juice

2 teaspoons freshly squeezed lemon juice

¹⁄₂ cup lard

3 tablespoons vegetable oil

Corn tortillas, warmed (see page 108), for serving

Chopped white onion, chopped fresh cilantro, salsa of choice, and lime wedges, for serving

If heaven exists, it's likely an all-you-can-eat buffet of pork fried in pork fat. (Remember, you're already dead, so there's no risk of heart attack.) Yes, you could make *carnitas* using vegetable oil instead of lard. But as they say, life is short. At the restaurant, we render the lard ourselves—something you can do if you can find extra-fatty pork. But for ready-to-go lard, check out your local butcher shop or Mexican market. Although any salsa will do, our chef Mike Garcia loves *carnitas* with chipotle-tomatillo salsa (page 30). He puts it simply: "It's one of my favorite flavor combos ever." For extra porkiness, sprinkle the top with crumbled bits of *chicharrónes* (fried pork rinds).

Put the pork in a nonreactive Dutch oven or other large, heavy pot with a lid. Add the onion, garlic, sugar, salt, oregano, bay leaf, orange juice, and lemon juice and toss to coat the meat evenly. Cover and refrigerate for at least 12 hours or up to 24 hours.

Bring the pork to room temperature. Heat the lard in a small pan over medium heat until it melts, then pour it over the pork. Cover the pot, place over medium-low heat, and cook the pork for about 3 hours, until the pork begins to pull apart easily when tested with a fork.

Remove from the heat. Using a slotted spoon, transfer the pork to a bowl. Discard the cooking liquid and clean the pot. Using a couple of forks, shred the pork a bit but not completely, removing any large chunks of fat.

Return the pot to the stove top over high heat and add the oil. At the minute the oil begins to smoke, using tongs or a spoon and working in batches to avoid crowding, carefully add some of the meat to the hot oil and cook, turning as needed, for about 4 minutes, until crisp on all sides. (If some onions are still attached, don't worry about it.)

Serve with the tortillas, onion, cilantro, salsa, and lime.

For the love of lard

Crisco is out. Lard is in. Although lard may still have the undeservedly bad rap that it started to develop in the 1950s when it was first tied it to heart disease, the pendulum is slowly swinging back in its favor. Lard has less saturated fat and more than twice the monounsaturated fat of butter.

If you're looking for the most healthful lard, don't look in the grocery store. Lard sold in a can has usually been hydrogenated to extend its shelf life. Look instead for leaf lard, which is the highest grade available. It comes from the soft fat around the loin and kidneys of the pig and has a neutral flavor. It is a great cooking fat with a high smoke point, which means you can really crank up the heat before your smoke alarm goes off. Look for it at your local butcher shop or order it online. Once you've tracked it down, it will keep in the refrigerator for up to a year.

Cochinita pibil taco

MAKES ABOUT 16 TACOS;
SERVES 4 TO 6

2 tablespoons vegetable oil

2 tablespoons achiote paste

¹/₂ cup freshly squeezed orange juice

¹/₂ cup freshly squeezed lime juice

6 cloves garlic, chopped

1¹/₂ tablespoons kosher salt

1¹/₂ teaspoons freshly ground black pepper

3 pounds boneless pork shoulder, in 2 equal-size pieces

2 large banana leaves

Corn tortillas, warmed (see page 108), for serving

Chopped white onion, chopped fresh cilantro, salsa of choice, and lime wedges, for serving

This achiote-stained pulled-pork specialty from the Yucatán has been modernized for everyday cooking. (Although if you want to stick to tradition and wrap a marinated suckling pig in banana leaves and cook it in a wood-fired earthen pit, we salute you.) Banana leaves impart an herbal fragrance to the meat (see page 200). However, we tested the pork covered with aluminum foil—which was decidedly less sexy—and the difference in flavor was subtle. Choose your own adventure. Either way, this dish is delicious. Traditionally the pork is served with Pickled red onions (page 41), but try it with an unconventional pairing of Cal-Mex corn salsa (page 36)—or both!

To make the marinade, in a blender, combine the oil, achiote paste, orange juice, lime juice, garlic, salt, and pepper and puree until smooth.

Put the pork in a large, heavy-duty zip-top plastic bag, add the marinade, and seal the bag closed. Massage the contents of the bag to evenly coat the pork with the marinade. Alternatively, place the pork in a glass or ceramic container, add the marinade, rub the marinade into the pork until it is well coated, and cover with plastic wrap. Marinate in the refrigerator for at least 8 hours or up to 24 hours, turning the pork a few times to marinate evenly.

Preheat the oven to 325°F. Remove the pork from the refrigerator.

Select a large roasting pan. To ready the banana leaves for lining the pan, first check for a hard part on each leaf where the leaf attaches to the rib, and cut it out with scissors. Next, cut each leaf into 3 equal sections, each about 12 inches longer than the length of the pan. Line the bottom and sides of the pan with the leaf sections, overlapping them and letting them hang over the edges of the pan. Remove the pork from the marinade and lay it in the pan, then pour the marinade over it. Fold the leaf overhang over the meat. Lay them over the top of the meat, again generously overlapping the edges, and tuck them in around the sides. Cover the pan loosely with aluminum foil.

Place in the oven and cook for about 4 hours, until the meat is thoroughly fork-tender.

To serve, transfer the pork to a large bowl. Pour the marinade in the pan into a separate bowl and spoon off any fat from the top. Using a couple of forks, shred the pork, discarding any meat that is too fatty. Pour the leftover marinade over the pork to taste, then taste the pork and season with salt if needed.

Serve with the tortillas, onion, cilantro, salsa, and lime.

Of pig and people: a pit master comes to Wine Country

For a number of years, the vast Culinary Institute of America (CIA) at Greystone in St. Helena, California—located in the middle of Napa's wine country—has been hosting its annual Worlds of Flavor conference. One of its first conferences focused on the cuisine of Mexico, and the CIA flew in native-born Silvio Campos, a master of Yucatecán pit cooking.

To prepare a pit for cooking, Campos typically lines it with stones and then builds a huge fire, which he then allows to burn down to hot coals (like 1000°F hot). The pit ready, he lays the leaves of fig and avocado trees on the coals, wraps banana leaves around the achiote-marinated pork, buries the wrapped pork in the pit, covers the pit with wet burlap bags, and then seals it with earth and lets the pork cook away.

So there was Campos roasting a pig on the grounds of the castlelike CIA facilities in fancy St. Helena. I'm sure he must have thought he was in a strange dream. After a delicious lunch of the moist, succulent shredded pork, Rick Bayless, the emcee of the event, invited Campos up to the stage for everyone to celebrate. As hundreds of people clapped enthusiastically, their bellies full, Campos wept with emotion. We all wiped away some tears, too. It was one of those we-are-the-world food moments that was unforgettable.

Mama Virginia's chile verde taco

Virginia Hinojosa, the true matron of our Valencia Street kitchen, does more than cook for us. She keeps our whole kitchen crew in line (which is how her nickname was born). One day, Virginia brought in her own delicious *chile verde* for us to sample. We had to have the recipe. Although we've tweaked it a bit, it's about as simple as can be: no browning of meat, no roasting of vegetables, just truly humble cooking with a lot of flavor. Once the meat is cooked, you will be left with a heavenly pork-and-chile-infused broth that we recommend you reserve for another use. You can turn it into a soup by adding some chicken broth, or try an easy riff on pozole by adding hominy and shredded cabbage.

In a large pot, combine the tomatillos, jalapeño chiles, and water and bring to a boil over high heat. Turn down the heat to a simmer, cover, and cook for 10 to 15 minutes, until the tomatillos and chiles are soft. Remove from the heat and let cool to room temperature.

Transfer the contents of the pot to a blender, add the garlic, chopped onion, cilantro, and salt, and process until smooth. If your blender is too small to accommodate everything in one batch, puree the ingredients in two batches.

Dry the pot, place it over medium heat, and add the oil. When the oil is hot, add the poblano chile and sliced onions and cook, stirring occasionally, for about 5 minutes, until the onions are softened. Add the pork, pour in the tomatillo-jalapeño mixture, and bring to a simmer. Turn down the heat to medium-low, cover, and simmer gently, stirring occasionally to prevent scorching, for 2 to 2 1/2 hours, until the pork is tender enough to pull apart with forks. Using a slotted spoon, transfer the pork to a bowl with some of its juice. Using a couple of forks, shred the meat into chunky pieces.

Serve with the tortillas, onion, cilantro, salsa, and lime.

**MAKES ABOUT 12 TACOS;
SERVES 6**

5 tomatillos, hulls removed and halved

2 jalapeño chiles, stemmed and halved

4 cups water

1 clove garlic, coarsely chopped

1/4 cup chopped yellow onion, plus 1 1/2 cups sliced

1/3 cup chopped fresh cilantro

1 1/2 tablespoons kosher salt

2 tablespoons vegetable oil

1 poblano chile, stemmed, seeded, and cut lengthwise into 1/2-inch-wide strips

2 1/2 pounds pork butt or shoulder, trimmed of fat and cut into 3-inch cubes

Corn tortillas, warmed (see page 108), for serving

Chopped white onion, chopped fresh cilantro, salsa of choice, and lime wedges, for serving

I'll have mine crispy: How to make tacos dorados (and instant friends)

Dorado *means "golden" in Spanish, which should give you a good hint that tacos dorados—generally filled with shredded meat—are crispy, fried bites of heaven. They're a bit of work, but they will make you very popular.*

Flautas are rolled into a "flute," but we prefer our tortillas simply folded in half before they hit the fryer. To make a taco dorado, pour peanut oil or another oil with a high smoke point to a depth of about 2 inches into a wide, heavy saucepan or deep sauté pan and heat to 350°F. Have a wire rack ready for draining the cooked tacos. Take your choice of braised meat from the taco recipes in this book, such as Guajillo-braised beef short rib (page 102), Shot-and-a-beer braised chicken (page 132), or Mama Virginia's chile verde (page 129), and use a slotted spoon to separate the meat from its juices. (If you're looking for a vegetarian version, try using the potato-and-greens filling for the empanadas on page 73.)

Put ¼ to ⅓ cup of the meat on a corn tortilla, fold the tortilla over into a half moon, and use tongs to carefully place it in the oil, taking care to avoid any splatter or let the filling spill out. (Tip: If your tortillas aren't pliable enough, warm them very briefly in the microwave.) Use the tongs to press down on the curved edge of the tortilla for a few seconds until the tortilla begins to crisp and seal the filling in place. Fill and add more tortillas to the hot oil, taking care not to crowd them in the pan. You can fry about 4 tacos at a time at the most. After about 2 minutes, or when the tortillas are golden and crisp, transfer the tacos to the wire rack to drain.

Serve the tacos hot topped with shredded iceberg lettuce, chopped tomatoes, and crema. We think tacos dorados work best with a classic hot sauce like Tapatío—that and a very cold beer. A Michelada (page 182) would be perfect.

Tacos dorados are crispy, fried bites of heaven. They're a bit of work, but they will make you very popular.

Shot-and-a-beer braised chicken taco

MAKES ABOUT 16 TACOS;
SERVES 4 TO 6

3 ancho chiles, stemmed
and seeded

2 dried chipotle chiles,
stemmed and seeded

^{1}/$_4$ cup vegetable oil, or
more if needed

3 pounds boneless,
skinless chicken thighs

1 yellow onion, chopped

1 habanero chile,
stemmed

3 cloves garlic, chopped

1 (12-ounce) can
favorite beer

1 shot (1^1/$_2$ ounces)
favorite tequila

1 cup chicken broth,
preferably low-sodium

1 cup diced
canned tomatoes

2 tablespoons kosher salt

1 tablespoon ground
cumin

1 tablespoon dried
Mexican oregano

Corn tortillas, warmed (see
page 108), for serving

Chopped white onion,
chopped fresh cilantro,
lime wedges, and salsa of
your choice for serving

In the restaurant industry, "a shot and a beer" is a standard bar order after a long night. In the case of this boozy braise, it's chicken that gets to drink up a splash of tequila and a can of Tecate. Note that the habanero is left whole to avoid getting capsaicin, the compound in chiles that carries the heat, on your fingers. The end result isn't terribly spicy, but if you want to take the fire down a notch, slip on some gloves and slice the habanero, removing the seeds and membranes, or omit it completely. You can also use bone-in chicken thighs; just pull the chicken off the bone before serving.

Toast the ancho and chipotle chiles in a dry, heavy skillet over medium heat, turning once, for about 30 seconds on each side, until fragrant but not blackened. Take care that they do not burn. Set aside.

Heat the oil in a Dutch oven or other large, heavy pot with a lid over medium-high heat. When the oil is hot, working in batches, add the chicken thighs and cook, turning once, for about 3 minutes on each side, until browned. Add an extra drizzle of oil if needed to prevent sticking. As the thighs are ready, transfer them to a plate and set aside.

Add the onion and habanero to the oil remaining in the pot and sauté over medium-high heat for about 5 minutes, until the onion is caramelized. Add the garlic and sauté for about 2 minutes. Add the toasted chiles, beer, tequila, broth, tomatoes, salt, cumin, and oregano, turn down the heat to medium-low, and simmer, uncovered, for about 15 minutes, until the chiles have completely softened. Remove from the heat and let cool slightly.

Preheat the oven to 325°F.

While the oven is heating, pour the chile mixture into a blender and process until almost completely smooth (a little texture is fine). Return the chicken to the pot and pour the pureed sauce evenly over the top.

Cover the pot, place in the oven, and cook for 2 hours. Remove the lid and continue to cook, stirring if necessary to prevent sticking, for 25 to 30 minutes, until the chicken is fork-tender. If the sauce starts to reduce too much and the chicken begins to stick, add a little water or broth. Remove from the oven and use tongs or a fork to loosely shred the chicken, leaving it in the sauce.

Serve with the tortillas, onion, cilantro, and lime.

Spring booty taco

As the seasons change, so does our vegetarian, market-inspired taco, though this recipe, due to popular demand, has become a spring staple. Even though Mexicans commonly eat lots of greens and wild mushrooms I doubt that you'd find this exact mix of vegetables folded into a taco in Mexico. Its simplistic nature allows for seamless ingredient substitutions. The oyster mushrooms can be replaced with cremini or button, and any small waxy potatoes will work if you can't find fingerlings. If the green garlic eludes you, you can replace it with a mixture of 1 1/2 teaspoons finely chopped garlic and 3 tablespoons thinly sliced green onion, adding it after the asparagus and mushrooms are cooked and then cooking for about 1 minute. Try this taco topped with our creamy Tomatillo-avocado salsa (page 26).

Fill a large saucepan three-fourths full with water and bring to a boil over high heat. While the water is heating, line a large plate with paper towels. When the water boils, add a generous pinch of salt and the potatoes and cook for about 7 minutes, until fork-tender. Drain the potatoes in a colander and place under cold running water for about 30 seconds. Transfer the potatoes to the lined plate to absorb any excess water.

Heat the oil in a large sauté pan over medium-high heat. Add the asparagus, mushrooms, and green garlic and cook, stirring occasionally, for about 5 minutes, until the mushrooms and asparagus are tender.

Add the potatoes and *recado*, mix well, and cook for 2 to 3 minutes longer to marry the flavors. Remove from the heat and season with salt.

Serve with the tortillas, onion, cilantro, salsa, and lime.

MAKES ABOUT 10 TACOS;
SERVES 4 TO 6

Kosher salt

1 cup sliced fingerling potatoes (1/4 inch thick)

2 tablespoons olive oil

1 1/2 cups cut-up asparagus (1/2-inch-long pieces)

1 cup coarsely chopped oyster mushrooms (1-inch pieces)

1/4 cup sliced green garlic (1/8 inch thick)

2 teaspoons El Jefe's glove-box recado (page 38)

Corn tortillas, warmed (see page 108), for serving

Chopped white onion, chopped fresh cilantro, salsa of choice, and lime wedges, for serving

Tangy achiote-rubbed grilled chicken taco

MAKES ABOUT 12 TACOS;
SERVES 4 TO 6

2 pounds skin-on,
boneless chicken thighs

2 tablespoons ground
annatto seeds

¹/₂ teaspoon ground
allspice

¹/₂ teaspoon ground
turmeric

2 tablespoons chile
powder (preferably árbol)

2 tablespoons kosher salt

2 tablespoons dried
Mexican oregano

2 teaspoons agave nectar

4 cloves garlic, crushed

²/₃ cup cider vinegar

¹/₄ cup freshly squeezed
orange juice

Corn tortillas, warmed (see
page 108), for serving

Avocado slices, chopped
white onion, chopped
fresh cilantro, salsa of
choice, and lime wedges,
for serving

The snap of vinegar comes through to meet a bit of heat from the garlic and chile in this excellent grilled chicken recipe. It doesn't need to stop at a taco. We've used the same marinade to great effect for a whole roasted chicken. The hard, little brick-red annatto seeds (also called achiote) impart a slightly peppery, earthy taste and a hint of yellow to the chicken. Look for them at Mexican markets in the spice section. To grind them, use a spice grinder or clean coffee grinder. If you're having a hard time sourcing annatto seeds, don't forgo making this recipe. It's tasty with or without them. We prefer this recipe with moist dark meat, but you can use chicken breast, taking care not to let it dry out.

Put the chicken in a large, heavy-duty zip-top plastic bag. In a small bowl, combine the annatto seeds, allspice, turmeric, chile powder, salt, oregano, agave nectar, garlic, vinegar, and orange juice and mix well. Add the spice mixture to the chicken and seal the bag closed. Massage the contents of the bag to coat both sides the chicken evenly with the marinade. Alternatively, put the chicken in a glass or ceramic bowl, add the spice mixture, turn the chicken to coat evenly, and cover with plastic wrap. Marinate in the refrigerator for at least 2 hours or up to overnight, turning the chicken a few times to marinate evenly.

Prepare a medium fire for direct-heat cooking in a grill. Bring the chicken thighs to room temperature and remove them from the marinade.

Place the chicken, skin side down, on the grill rack directly over the fire and cook, turning after about 10 minutes. Cook for another 10 minutes on the other side. If the chicken is starting to burn or cook too quickly, move to a part of the grill with indirect heat and continue to cook. The chicken is done when an instant-read thermometer inserted into the thickest part registers 165°F.

Transfer the chicken to a cutting board and chop into small pieces, leaving the skin on (that's the tastiest part!). Serve the chicken with the tortillas, avocado, chopped onion, cilantro, salsa, and lime.

Chile powder: make your own

Chili powder, which varies from producer to producer, is generally a blend of one or more dried chiles mixed with spices and herbs. Chile (notice the *i* is swapped for an *e*) powder is one or more types of chile with no additions. Both are easy to make yourself. For chile powder, use your favorite whole dried chile variety or tinker with a few different varieties, such as ancho, cascabel, and árbol, in different ratios. Always stem and seed the chiles and toast them in a dry, heavy skillet over medium heat until fragrant before grinding them. For chili powder, add some toasted cumin seeds, toasted dried oregano, and/or garlic powder and grind everything together. The result will taste fresher than anything you can buy.

Baja-style fish taco

Nothing beats the juxtaposition of something soft wrapped around something crunchy and fried: think tempura sushi, fried-chicken sandwiches, and yes, fish tacos. Light as air but crisp as can be, this is the ultimate beer-based fish-taco batter. Although the fish tastes best fresh out of the hot oil, you can put the first few batches on a baking sheet in a 250°F oven until you're done frying the rest. If you would prefer something a bit lighter, these tacos are also great with grilled fish.

Sprinkle the fish pieces on both sides with the salt and set aside. Pour the oil to a depth of 1 1/2 inches into a deep, heavy pot and heat to 350°F. Line a baking sheet with paper towels.

While the oil is heating, make the batter. In a bowl, stir together the flour, baking powder, and salt. Gradually add the beer and stir until smooth.

To cook the fish, work in batches so as not to crowd the pieces in the oil. Using tongs, dip each piece of fish into the batter, letting the excess drain off, and carefully submerge it in the hot oil. Fry for 2 to 3 minutes, until golden brown and cooked through. Using the tongs, transfer the fish to the lined baking sheet and season with salt.

Serve with the tortillas, *crema*, cabbage, cilantro, lime, and your choice of salsa.

The best fish for frying

The best fish to use for tacos is something mild, chunky, flaky, and white. An oily fish like salmon will leave you with pieces of fish that will not get crisp and will double the richness rating. Although we suggest rock cod, mahimahi fits the bill, too, as does halibut or snapper.

MAKES ABOUT 12 TACOS;
SERVES 4 TO 6

1 1/4 pounds rock cod or other mild white fish fillets (see note), cut into 4 by 1 1/2-inch pieces

1 tablespoon kosher salt

Vegetable oil, for deep-frying

Batter

1 1/2 cups plus 3 tablespoons all-purpose flour

3 1/4 teaspoons baking powder

4 teaspoons kosher salt

1 (12-ounce) can light-bodied beer, such as Tecate

For Serving

Corn tortillas, warmed (see page 108)

1 1/2 cups crema, homemade (page 37) or store-bought

3 cups shredded green or purple cabbage

1/4 cup loosely packed chopped fresh cilantro

12 lime wedges

Salsa of your choice

Puerto Nuevo–style lobster taco

6 live lobsters (spiny
Pacific or Maine)

1/2 cup salted butter, cut
into cubes

1 teaspoon minced garlic

1 teaspoon freshly
squeezed lime juice, or
more to taste

Kosher salt

Not really refried beans
(page 92)

Lazy salsa (page 28), fresh
version

About 12 small flour
tortillas, warmed
(see page 108)

The right lobster (or prawn) for the job

The spiny lobster is a
claw-free distant cousin
to the Maine lobster
and a solidly sustainable
choice, with a season
that runs from October
to March. (If you don't
have local access,
catalinaop.com will ship
it to you.) Maine lobster
works well, too, as will
large raw prawns. Simply
broil them in the shell
(the shell keeps the
juices in) and let your
guests shell them at
the table.

Throughout Joe's childhood, he and his uncle would take off on weekends and drive from Laguna Beach, California, to Puerto Nuevo, Mexico, a town famous for its spiny lobster. In Puerto Nuevo, restaurants serve a platter of lobster tails that have been fried in lard, accompanied with a little bowl of drawn butter, refried beans, rice, and warm flour tortillas. Although Joe returned to this border town not long ago to find it dishearteningly touristy, his memory of that delicious combination lives on. This is our lard-free version of it (though we are definitely not opposed to lard, see page 125). If you're looking for a little crunch, some cabbage or Pickled red onions (page 41) would make a nice addition.

Fill a large stockpot two-thirds full with water and bring to a boil over high heat. Plunge 2 lobsters into the boiling water and cook for 3 minutes (the lobsters will not be fully cooked). Using tongs, transfer the lobsters to a colander, then run cold water over them to arrest the cooking. Repeat with the remaining 4 lobsters in two batches.

Working with 1 lobster at a time, turn the lobster belly up. Using a large, heavy knife or cleaver, place the tip of the blade in the center of the lobster and cut in half lengthwise from the center to the end of the head. Then cut in the other direction from the center through the tail. Remove the intestinal tract and rinse away the green tomalley.

Position a rack on the top level of the oven and preheat the broiler. In a small saucepan, melt the butter over low heat and swirl in the garlic and lime juice. Season with salt and taste and add more lime juice if desired.

Place the lobster halves, meat side up, on 2 large rimmed baking sheets. Brush the meat with some of the butter. Slip a pan under the broiler and broil for 2 to 3 minutes, just until the meat is opaque. Repeat with the second pan.

Serve the lobsters with the beans, the salsa, the remaining warm butter, and the tortillas. Invite diners to assemble their own tacos or to eat the lobsters directly from the shell. It's a mix-and-match eating experience at its best.

Lone Star breakfast taco

Our hometown of San Francisco doesn't seem to share Austin's affinity for the breakfast taco, but it's something every city should get on board with. Pledging allegiance to Texas, we serve these in flour tortillas, but corn tortillas would be equally good. Be sure to place a *salsa picante* like Tapatío or, as a nod to the South, the more vinegary Tabasco at the table.

Place the poblano chiles directly over the flame of a gas burner and turn with tongs for about 3 minutes, until charred and blistered all over. Alternatively, place the chiles in a dry, heavy skillet over high heat and turn with tongs for about 3 minutes, until charred and blistered all over. Transfer the chiles to a bowl, cover with plastic wrap, and let steam for 10 minutes. Remove the chiles and gently peel or scrape away the skin. Slice each chile in half lengthwise, remove the stem and seeds, and cut into strips 1 inch long by 1/8 inch wide. Measure out 1/3 cup. Set the rest aside for another day.

Put the bacon in a large, heavy skillet over medium heat and leave to cook for a few minutes, until some of the fat has rendered. Using a slotted spoon, transfer the bacon to a plate. Add the potatoes to the pan and cook, stirring occasionally, for about 10 minutes, until cooked through. Add the onion and return the bacon to the pan. Cook, stirring occasionally, for another few minutes, until the bacon is cooked and the onion is soft.

Turn down the heat to low. Add the eggs, chiles, and cheese and stir for a few minutes until the eggs are gently scrambled (taking care not to overcook) and the cheese is melted. Season with salt. Remove from the heat.

One at a time, warm the flour tortillas directly over the low flame of a gas burner for 10 to 15 seconds on each side, until puffed. Alternatively, warm them in a heavy, dry skillet over low heat on both sides for about the same amount of time.

Serve the eggs with the tortillas, cilantro, and hot sauce.

MAKES 6 FILLING TACOS;
SERVES 6

2 small poblano chile peppers

3 slices thick-cut bacon, cut into 1-inch pieces

5 small new potatoes (about 8 ounces total), cut into 1/4-inch cubes

3/4 cup chopped yellow onion

6 eggs, whisked

1 cup shredded Monterey Jack cheese

Kosher salt

6 small flour tortillas

Chopped fresh cilantro and hot sauce, for serving

Flour tortillas: the good, the bad, the ugly

There are flour tortillas (more often than not puffy, dry, and, for lack of a better description, floury), and then there are *flour tortillas*. Any flour tortilla that deserves to be italicized will have a glossy sheen and an almost buttery aroma, appear a tiny bit transparent, and become almost flaky when heated.

Cashew Crema

²/₃ cup raw cashews

1 teaspoon cumin seeds

6 tablespoons freshly
squeezed lime juice (from
about 3 limes)

¹/₄ cup water

2 teaspoons kosher salt

Pumpkin Seeds

2 teaspoons vegetable oil

¹/₃ cup raw hulled
pumpkin seeds

¹/₄ teaspoon cayenne
pepper

¹/₄ teaspoon kosher salt

Filling

2 tablespoons
vegetable oil

³/₄ cup finely chopped
yellow onion

1 clove garlic, minced

3 cups ¹/₂-inch-diced
butternut squash

1 teaspoon chile powder

2 teaspoons kosher salt

4 cups finely chopped kale

Corn tortillas, warmed (see
page 108), for serving

Chopped white onion,
chopped fresh cilantro,
and salsa of choice, for
serving (optional)

Continued

Butternut squash, kale, and crunchy pepitas taco

Drummed up by our intrepid recipe tester Lauren Godfrey, this nontraditional taco, sweet with squash, earthy and nutty with kale, and crunchy with fried pumpkin seeds (*pepitas*), is—*shhhhh*—vegan. Don't tell anyone, but because it is so tasty, no one will care. The cashew *crema* can be replaced by store-bought *crema* or our Cumin-lime crema (page 37), but after polling both vegetarian and carnivorous friends, everyone preferred the nutty and rich nondairy cashew version (which must be made with raw cashews to work). To prepare the butternut squash, use a sharp peeler to remove the tough skin before slicing it in half and scooping out the seeds and fibers. Lazy cook's tip: Some markets sell butternut squash already peeled and seeded and ready to go.

To make the *crema*, soak the raw cashews in room-temperature water to cover for at least 1 hour. Drain and reserve.

Toast the cumin in a small, dry, heavy skillet over medium heat for about 1 minute, until fragrant. Transfer to a spice grinder, let cool, and grind finely.

In a blender, combine the cashews, cumin, lime juice, water, and salt. Start the blender on the lowest speed and gradually increase to the highest speed. Blend for at least 1 minute, until a creamy consistency. Pour into a serving bowl and set aside.

To make the pumpkin seeds, heat the oil in a heavy skillet over medium heat. When the oil is hot, add the pumpkin seeds and sauté for about 2 minutes, taking care that they do not burn. The seeds will begin to puff up and pop. Once they appear toasted, immediately pour them into a bowl. Toss with the cayenne and salt and set aside.

To make the filling, heat the oil in a large, heavy skillet over medium heat. Add the onion and sauté for about 3 minutes, until softened. Add the garlic and sauté for about 1 minute more. Add the squash and sauté for 6 to 7 minutes, just until the squash begins to soften. Season with the chile powder and salt.

Butternut squash, kale, and crunchy pepitas taco

Add the kale and cook, stirring, for about 1 minute, until it begins to wilt. Remove from the heat, taste, and adjust the seasoning with salt if needed.

Serve with the tortillas, *crema*, pumpkin seeds, onion, cilantro, and salsa. To assemble each taco, invite guests to spoon about ½ cup of the warm filling into a tortilla and top with some *crema* and pumpkin seeds. If guests want more toppings, they can finish off their tacos with onion, cilantro, and salsa.

The vegetarian Mexican

Anyone who says that Mexican food is unhealthy has not been to Mexico. It's the United States, where Mexican-American combo platters oozing with fried things and cheese are often the norm, that has it all wrong. In this cookbook, health enthusiasts and vegetarians have plenty to choose from. Take a look at the following recipes and make a menu to your liking.

Butternut squash, kale, and crunchy pepitas taco (page 145)*

Nopal, egg, and tomato taco (page 147)

Spring booty taco (page 133)*

Quesadilla with squash blossoms, sweet peppers, and goat cheese (page 72)

Flaky potato-and-greens empanadas with salsa verde (page 73)

Chile con queso (page 52)

Cebollitas (page 96)*

Grilled corn on the cob with glove-box recado (page 57)*

Classic guacamole (page 53)*

Not really refried beans (page 92)*

Rice-o-licious (page 90)*

*Completely vegan!

Nopal, egg, and tomato taco

Nopales, or fresh cactus paddles, are the star of this mild-mannered, easy-to-make taco that's great for breakfast or lunch. They can be found, thorns removed and sometimes prechopped, in the produce aisle of most Mexican markets. Although you can serve it with any one of our salsas, we really like this taco with a dash of hot sauce such as Tapatío. Eggs are a great match for corn or flour tortillas, so take your pick. Try substituting El Jefe's glove-box recado (page 38) for the cumin.

Bring a saucepan three-fourth full of water to a boil and add the salt. Add the nopal and cook for about 2 minutes, until crisp-tender. Drain in a colander and let sit for 10 minutes.

Heat the oil in a nonstick skillet over medium heat. Add the onion and garlic and sprinkle in the cumin. Cook for about a minute, or until the onion and garlic are soft. Add the tomato and nopal and sauté for another minute, until the nopal is cooked but not totally soft. Add the eggs and cook, stirring, for about 2 minutes (taking care not to overcook), until the eggs are gently scrambled. Remove from the heat and season with salt.

Serve with the tortillas, onion, cilantro, *queso fresco*, and hot sauce.

MAKES 6 TACOS; SERVES 6

1 teaspoon kosher salt

1 cup diced nopal

1 tablespoon vegetable oil

$^1/_2$ cup finely chopped yellow onion

2 cloves garlic, minced

$^1/_2$ teaspoon ground cumin

$^1/_2$ cup diced tomato

6 eggs, whisked

Kosher salt

Corn or small flour tortillas, warmed (see page 108), for serving

Chopped white onion, chopped fresh cilantro, crumbled queso fresco (optional), and hot sauce, for serving

La Taquiza

The ultimate DIY taco party

Taquiza menu for twelve

Imagine a table decked out with a tempting spread of **taco fillings**, a stack of warm tortillas, and salsas galore. Add a pitcher of margaritas, invite your friends, and you've got the ultimate *taquiza*, or make-your-own taco fiesta.

Once you get the hang of a *taquiza*, the mix-and-match options are limitless: you can go all vegetarian, or make it a carnivore's delight. But the best *taquiza* menu offers a balanced bit of this and of that, allowing fickle guests to make tacos to their liking.

The key to carrying off a truly festive taco party without sweating it too much is to select recipes that allow you to space out the preparation times. Although you can serve grilled or sautéed fillings, braises will save you a lot of hassle, because they can be prepared a day or two in advance and kept warm on the stove top as the party goes on. On the following pages we provide instructions for what we consider an intermediate-level *taquiza* menu. You can always delete dishes or add more, depending on your ambitions.

The more the merrier: making pitcher drinks

No *taquiza* would be complete without an icy pitcher of cocktails. To make enough to serve a crowd, you can take any of the cocktails that apear in the last chapter (starting on page 171) and multiply the recipes as needed. Here are two ways to make pitcher-size cocktails for a crowd.

The cool-bartender way

To make pitcher cocktails at the restaurant, we fill two cocktail shakers with ice. In each one, we put double the amount for each ingredient of a single-serving cocktail, shake, and strain into an ice-filled pitcher. This makes four servings that stay nice and cold. (If you really want to impress your friends, vigorously shake both cocktail shakers simultaneously over your head while looking very serious. Maybe get a tattoo and grow a beard.) Serve.

The easy-way-out way

Multiply the amount of each ingredient in the cocktail recipe by the number of people you intend to serve at once (taking into account how big your pitcher is). To ensure the best result—assuming it's a cold drink—chill all of the ingredients beforehand. Mix everything together at once in a pitcher filled with ice. Serve.

Up to one month before the party

Prepare and freeze the Guajillo-braised beef short rib and Mama Virginia's chile verde.

Two days before the party

Prepare and refrigerate the Chile con queso.

One day before the party

Prepare and refrigerate the Just-hot-enough habanero salsa and the Not really refried beans.

The day of the party

Prepare the Pickled red onions and the Lazy salsa. Mix the two cocktails in pitchers and refrigerate (do not add ice).

Just before the party starts

- Chop the cilantro and onions and cut the lime wedges. Put in separate bowls.

- Put the salsas and pickled onions in serving bowls.

- Warm the braised meats over low heat on the stove top. Ladle some of each meat into a serving bowl with a lid and place the bowls on the table. Keep the remaining meat simmering over very low heat on the stove, for refilling the bowls as needed.

- Heat the tortillas and keep them warm in a large tortilla warmer or in aluminum foil (see page 108 for warming suggestions).

- Warm the Chile con queso and transfer it to a serving bowl at the last minute.

- To keep it from browning, prepare the guacamole just before your guests arrive.

- Set out a bucket of ice, a dozen tumblers, and the two pitchers of cocktails. Let your guests serve themselves. (If your cocktail recipe of choice calls for salted rims, you can presalt the rims, let your guests do it themselves, or just forget that step altogether.)

- Put the chips on the table.

- Turn on the music. Remove your apron and pour yourself a drink.

Twenty 20-minute (max) tacos del día:
Quick inspirations for what to wrap in a tortilla

It's liberating to realize that tacos are essentially anything you can wrap a fresh tortilla around. Every week, Tacolicious serves up a different special taco, and years in, we've barely scratched the surface of all that's out there. Although plenty of traditional combinations exist for you to try, this is the moment we encourage you to shed the yoke of "authenticity." If you've got leftovers—or a little ingenuity—it's likely that you've got a delicious taco filling in your pantry or refrigerator.

1. The pilgrim's delight

Shred leftover roasted turkey. Season with a bit of salt. Add a swipe of refried beans to a tortilla, top with the turkey, plus pickled onions, avocado slices, and cilantro. Crumble *queso fresco* on top.

2. Balls of fire

Take Albóndigas in tomato-chipotle sauce (page 80) and quarter a meatball. Top with chopped onion, pickled jalapeños, and crumbled *queso fresco*. Drizzle with more of the chipotle sauce and serve.

3. Hurrah for rajas

Heat a little vegetable oil in a skillet. Add chopped garlic and onion slices and sauté until softened. Add strips of roasted poblano chiles (see page 143), plus a dollop of *crema* and some shredded Oaxaca cheese. Season with salt. Let it cook until bubbly. Serve hot in a corn or flower tortilla.

4. Fried on the inside

Take fried chicken and chop roughly. (If the chicken isn't already warm, heat a little oil in a skillet and toss the chicken in the pan until hot and crispy.) Serve with finely shredded cabbage and a drizzle of Cumin-lime crema (page 37). Pickled jalapeños would be a good addition, too.

5. Cali cheesesteak

Heat some vegetable oil in a skillet over low heat, add a sliced onion, and cook for about 15 minutes, until nice and caramelized. Add very thinly sliced flank steak and cook briefly to brown. Season with salt. Serve the steak and onion topped with Chile con queso (page 52).

6. Chicken bánh mì

Take shredded roasted chicken and top it with shredded carrots and daikon, coarsely chopped cilantro, jalapeño slices, and a drizzle of mayo mixed with Sriracha sauce to taste.

7. BLAT

Place coarsely chopped thick-cut fried bacon in a tortilla with chopped tomatoes, shredded lettuce, and Classic guacamole (page 53). Drizzle with *crema* and add chopped cilantro.

8. Crispy pig

Heat a little vegetable oil in a skillet. Add one recipe's worth of the Smoky chipotle-tomatillo salsa (page 30) to the pan and bring to a simmer. Add bite-size chunks of *chicharrón* and cook until slightly softened. Serve with chopped onion and cilantro, some avocado slices, and a squeeze of lime.

9. K-pop

Go out for Korean barbecue. Bring home leftover bulgogi (grilled marinated beef). Warm it briefly. Swipe a tortilla with gochujang (Korean chile paste) and add the beef. Top with a drizzle of sesame oil and some kimchi, chopped green onion, and chopped cilantro.

10. Shrimp off a stick

Thread a bunch of peeled medium-size shrimp onto a few skewers. Grill the shrimp over a medium-hot fire. Remove the shrimp from the skewers and toss them in a bowl with a little El Jefe's glove-box recado (page 38), taking into account that it's very salty, and a squeeze of lime. Serve with shredded cabbage, *crema*, chopped cilantro, and a dash of hot sauce.

11. Wild at heart

Take any assortment of wild mushrooms, such as chanterelles, porcini, and morels, and sauté in a little butter. Add chopped shallots, garlic, and serrano chiles. Season with salt. Serve topped with chopped cilantro, crumbled *queso fresco*, and a squeeze of lime.

12. Short-order breakfast

Fry chopped onion with Mexican chorizo. Add eggs and scramble. Toss in chopped cilantro just before the eggs have set. Serve with hot sauce.

13. Beans and bacon

Add diced thick-cut bacon to a cold skillet. Turn on the heat to medium and cook the bacon until crispy. Add finely chopped onion and jalapeños and cook a minute more. Then stir in pinto beans or black beans and heat through. Add shredded Oaxaca cheese and heat until melted. Season with salt. Serve topped with chopped cilantro and onion. Or finish with Pickled red onions (page 41).

14. Spicy crabby

Heat a little vegetable oil in a skillet. Add chopped onion and celery and sauté until soft. Add a bit of chopped habanero chile, then throw in as much fresh-cooked flaked crabmeat as you can afford. Cook just until the crabmeat warms. Toss with chopped cilantro and finish with a squeeze of lime.

15. Summer's on

Heat a little olive oil in a skillet. Add chopped onion and sauté until soft. Add any type of diced summer squash (zucchini, crookneck, pattypan) and cook just until softened (don't overcook), then stir in fresh corn kernels. Toss with a tiny bit of chopped mint, cilantro, and basil. Serve with or without crumbled *queso fresco*. Pickled red onions (page 41) would be a nice addition.

16. Chinese takeout

Find a Chinese deli that sells great roasted duck. Bring it home, bone it, coarsely chop it, leaving the skin on, and then warm it. Swipe a flour tortilla with hoisin sauce, add some duck, and top with green onions sliced into strips and a drizzle of Sriracha sauce. Chopped cilantro and a squeeze of lime would be good here, too.

17. Winter's greens

Bring a large pot filled with water to a boil. Boil any mixture of greens until just tender (Swiss chard, spinach, and dandelion greens are ready quickly; heartier greens like dinosaur kale and collards will take longer), then drain well and chop. Heat a good amount of olive oil in a skillet. Add a hefty dose of chopped garlic and a sprinkle of red pepper flakes and sauté for a few minutes, until fragrant. Stir in the greens, heat through, and season with salt. Serve with cheese such as crumbled *queso fresco* or, if you're vegan, don't.

18. Cuban picadillo

Heat a little oil in a skillet. Add chopped onion and garlic and sauté until soft. Add ground beef and continue to cook. Add a good pinch of ground cinnamon and of cayenne pepper and a tiny pinch of ground cloves and cook until the beef is nearly cooked. Mix in a little canned pureed tomato and let cook for few minutes more. Add a scattering of dried currants or raisins and sliced green olives and throw in some slivered almonds, if you like. Season with salt.

19. The king of salmon

Place a thick fillet of the best salmon you can get your hands on, skin side down, on a hot grill. Season liberally with salt and pepper. Grill for about 8 minutes and flip. Cook for another 8 minutes, until just cooked through. Transfer to a cutting board, toss the skin, and coarsely chop the salmon. Serve topped with Cal-Mex corn salsa (page 36) and a squeeze of lime.

20. Quickie fajitas

Season thin slices of flank steak or chicken thigh with a little El Jefe's glove-box recado (page 38). Heat a skillet over hight heat. Add a little vegetable oil and sear sliced onion and green bell pepper. Add the beef or chicken slices and toss until cooked through. Serve with a dollop of sour cream or *crema* and a drizzle of Lazy salsa (page 28) or of a hot sauce like Tapatío. Flour tortillas are a must.

cocktails, aguas frescas + more

Tacos and margaritas go hand in hand for a reason. Casual and easygoing, they both encourage a let-the-good-times-roll attitude. At Tacolicious, all of our drinks fall in line with this life philosophy. (Come to think of it, pretty much everything we do at the restaurant falls in this line.) This approach yields the opposite of the heady concoctions currently favored by the mixology world, where brow-creasing brown spirits and tinctures of obscure liqueurs reign supreme. We staunchly believe that chile-laced food demands to be paired with something bright and refreshing, whether or not it's made with booze. This is why we prefer our cocktails and drinks to be light on their feet, made with minimal ingredients, fresh juices, and lots of ice.

That's not to say that we don't have a few tricks up our sleeve. Before you take on any of the following recipes, be sure to read them through. Some call for a little spoonful of fruit salsa, others for a dash of chile-spiked vinegar or a festive bit of cinnamon-laced agave syrup, and still others for a flavored salt–coated glass rim. All of these additions contribute to the traditional sweet-salty-tart flavor profile of Mexican cocktails (classics such as the Paloma and the Margarita are excellent examples).

Even more of these drinks call for tequila that has been infused with habanero chile or pineapple. (If you don't have the time to create an infusion, plain tequila will usually make a fine—though not quite as

fine—substitute.) As for what kind of tequila? Overall, we recommend using a good-quality 100 percent agave *blanco*, or white (also known or *plata*, or silver) tequila. Although the richer *reposado* (rested) and *añejo* (aged) tequilas make interesting cocktails, too, we generally like them for sipping (see pages 188–91).

For those of you who prefer to go alcohol free, there are plenty of juice-forward refreshers here to satisfy anyone—from kids to teetotalers—looking for a sophisticated cocktail substitute.

How to rim a glass with salt

Many of our cocktails call for dusting the rim of the glass with plain kosher salt or a flavored salt, which is easy to do. Cover a small plate with a shallow layer of the requested salt. Dampen the outside edge of the glass rim with a little water, citrus juice (you can just rub a wedge of a lime or lemon around the rim), or other complementary liquid and then, holding the glass rim at a slight angle, slowly rotate the outside edge through the salt, covering about 1/8 inch of the rim and gently shaking off the excess. If you find a full rim of salt to be too much, coat only half of the rim—or leave the salt off altogether.

To store the flavored salts, transfer them to an airtight container and store in the cupboard for up to 3 months.

Pasión (page 172)

Michelada (page 182)

Syrups, salts, and infusions

Although these concoctions are all used in the following cocktail or drink recipes, with a little imagination, they would brighten up any drink, tequila based or even alcohol free. Think of them as your flamboyant accessories—your secret weapons—to a basic bar set-up.

Agave syrup

The agave plant is kind to us. Not only does it provide us with the base for tequila, but it also makes a perfectly natural sweetener called agave nectar, one that we use to enliven all of our cocktails. (We like Simple Agave brand, an all-natural raw product made from blue agave; available at simpleagave.com.) Agave nectar is incredibly sweet, so it must be mixed with equal parts water, in the same way that sugar and water are combined to make simple syrup. You can mix up just the amount of agave syrup you need for one drink, but it's much easier to keep a bottle of diluted agave nectar on hand. That way, you'll have the syrup ready to go when the party starts. If you decide against mixing up a big batch, you can replace the 1 ounce agave syrup in any drink recipe with 1/2 ounce agave nectar mixed with 1/2 ounce warm water.

MAKES 2 CUPS

1 cup agave nectar
1 cup warm water

Mix together and strain through a fine-mesh sieve into a glass container with an airtight top. Store in the refrigerator. It should last indefinitely.

Cinnamon-and-chile agave syrup

This syrup adds a cozy, wintry heat to any cocktail or nonalcoholic drink. Although we use it our El sangre (page 181), you might try using it to sweeten warm apple cider spiked with tequila or the booze of your choice. On the nonalcoholic side, use it to sweeten a frothy hot cocoa made with Mexican chocolate.

MAKES 2 CUPS

1 cup water
1 tablespoon ground cinnamon
1 1/2 teaspoons cayenne pepper
1 cup agave nectar

In a saucepan, combine the water, cinnamon, and cayenne, bring to a simmer over medium heat, and simmer for 15 minutes. Remove from the heat and stir in the agave nectar. Set aside and let cool.

Strain through a fine-mesh sieve into a glass container with an airtight top. Store in the refrigerator for up to 1 month.

Pink peppercorn salt

We use this for our Margarita picante (page 171) and Paloma (page 172), but its mellow hit of pepper would suit most any cocktail that calls for a salted rim.

MAKES A SCANT ½ CUP

¼ cup pink peppercorns
2 tablespoons kosher salt
1 tablespoon sugar

Put the peppercorns in a spice grinder and grind finely. Sift through a fine-mesh sieve into a bowl, discarding the pink hulls captured in the sieve. Add the salt and the sugar and stir to mix well.

Chile salt

We like to rub rims with a lemon wedge before dipping them in this salt, which coats the rim of our El sangre cocktail (page 181), but would also be great on our Margarita picante (page 171) or Michelada (page 182).

MAKES A SCANT ½ CUP

4 tablespoons kosher salt
1 tablespoon sweet paprika
1 tablespoon cayenne pepper
1 tablespoon chile powder

In a small bowl, whisk together the salt, paprika, cayenne, and chili powder, mixing well.

Toasted-coconut salt

If you don't think salt, sugar, and coconut belong together, just imagine being on the white-sand beaches of Mexico, the salt from a dip in the ocean intermingling with your sweet tropical drink—or something to that effect. Trust us on this one. Use it with our Mucho gusto (page 178), or try it on the rim of a traditional piña colada.

MAKES ABOUT ¾ CUP

½ cup unsweetened shredded dried coconut
¼ cup sugar
2 tablespoons kosher salt

Preheat the oven to 350°F.

In a small bowl, stir together the coconut and sugar. Spread the coconut mixture evenly on a small rimmed baking pan, place in the oven, and toast, stirring every minute or so, for about 7 minutes, until lightly golden. Remove from the oven and let cool completely.

In a food processor, combine the coconut-sugar mixture and the salt and pulse for about 1 minute, until coarsely ground. Taste for a good sweet-salty balance and add more salt if needed.

Chile vinegar

Although this recipe is used in our Margarita picante (page 171), it would give a nice slap in the face to our Michelada (page 182) in place of the lime juice and chiles. Try adding a dash to a Bloody Maria (page 186), too.

MAKES ABOUT ¹/₂ CUP

¹/₄ cup red pepper flakes

¹/₂ cup rice vinegar

Combine the pepper flakes and vinegar in a small saucepan, bring to a boil over high heat, then lower to a simmer and cook for 5 minutes. Remove from the heat and let cool completely. Strain through a fine-mesh sieve and use immediately or store in an airtight container in the refrigerator for up to a month.

Apple-ginger cocktail salsa

We spoon this salsa on top of our nonalcoholic drink Mia (page 198), but it was originally served atop our sangria. If you're going to go this latter route, try a sangria with rosé, which lightens up the color and taste. In the winter, toss in some pomegranate seeds.

MAKES ABOUT 1¼ CUPS

1/2 cup 1/4-inch-diced tart apple such as Granny Smith

3/4 cup 1/4-inch-diced, peeled jicama

2 Fresno chiles, stemmed, seeded, and finely chopped

1 tablespoon finely chopped, peeled fresh ginger

2 tablespoons finely chopped lemon zest

2 tablespoons finely chopped orange zest

1/4 cup freshly squeezed orange juice

1/4 cup freshly squeezed lemon juice

In a bowl large enough to toss the ingredients freely, combine all of the ingredients and toss until evenly mixed. Use immediately or cover and refrigerate for up to 1 week.

Cucumber juice

No, cucumber juice isn't just for ladies who lunch. It also makes a great, appealingly delicate cocktail, such as If Honey could drink (page 178).

MAKES ABOUT ⅔ CUP

1 English cucumber, unpeeled and cubed

1/4 cup water

In a blender, combine the cucumber and water and blend just enough to liquefy. Strain through a fine-mesh sieve or through cheesecloth, discarding the solids. Use the juice immediately.

Hibiscus tea

In Mexico, tart hibiscus flowers, known as *flor de Jamaica*, are combined with agave syrup and lemon to make a wonderfully refreshing drink. For our Flor de Jamaica (page 181), we shake this tea with tequila, resulting in a hibiscus margarita.

MAKES ABOUT 3½ CUPS

2 cups dried hibiscus flowers

4 cups water

Combine the flowers and water in a saucepan and bring to a boil over high heat. Lower the heat to medium and simmer, uncovered, for 20 minutes.

Remove from the heat and let cool to room temperature. Strain through a fine-mesh sieve into an airtight glass container. Refrigerate for up to 1 week.

Infused tequilas

If you're a cocktail geek—and even if you're not—infusing tequila can provide a mad-scientist kind of entertainment. You can play around with all sorts of fruits, herbs, and even spices, mixed with different levels of aged tequila. Think oranges, grapefruit, cucumber, or cilantro. How long should you let the tequila sit before straining it? Check on your concoction daily (or hourly if you're tinkering with chiles) and make an executive decision. Truly, it's a matter of taste.

Habanero-infused tequila

Once this firewater is safely in the bottle, be sure to attach a label that warns the user about the heat.

MAKES ABOUT 3 CUPS

1 (750 ml) bottle 100 percent agave tequila, preferably blanco

6 habanero chiles, halved lengthwise

Combine the tequila and chiles in a glass bowl or jar and let sit for 1 hour. Strain the tequila through a fine-mesh sieve into a pitcher, then pour back into the tequila bottle and cap tightly.

Pineapple-infused tequila

After lime (the obvious choice), there might be no better match for tequila than pineapple. Its sweet yet zingy qualities stand up to tequila's own zestiness.

MAKES ABOUT 3 CUPS

1 (750 ml) bottle 100 percent agave tequila, preferably blanco

1 pineapple, peeled and cubed

Combine the tequila and pineapple in a glass bowl or jar, cover, and allow to infuse at room temperature for 4 days. Strain the tequila through a fine-mesh sieve into a pitcher, then pour back into the tequila bottle and cap tightly.

Cocktails

Yes, these are almost all tequila-based cocktails (with a couple rogue ones thrown in for the haters)—but hey, we're tequila lovers and we're not afraid to show it. And because Mexican food demands an endless summer attitude, almost every cocktail here is served over ice.

The Tacolicious margarita

When we first opened, we used Triple Sec to sweeten this classic cocktail, but today, we use agave syrup, which keeps the whole cocktail, barring the lime juice, in the agave family. We recommend it. Try making a margarita with both *blanco* and *reposado* tequilas and decide which one you prefer. The former makes a bright-tasting cocktail while the latter results in a warmer, cozier drink.

Coat the rim of a 10-ounce tumbler with the salt (see page 158). Fill the tumbler and a cocktail shaker with ice. Add the tequila, lime juice, and agave syrup to the cocktail shaker and shake vigorously. Strain into the tumbler. Garnish with the lime wedge and serve.

SERVES 1

Kosher salt, for coating glass rim

Ice

2 ounces 100 percent agave tequila

1 1/2 ounces freshly squeezed lime juice

1 ounce agave syrup (page 163)

1 lime wedge

Margarita picante

When you're in the market for a margarita with a kick, this one, spiked with chile vinegar, is a good choice. Although at the restaurant we serve it with a pink peppercorn salt rim, plain kosher salt is good, too.

Coat the rim of a 10-ounce tumbler with the salt (see page 158). Fill the tumbler and a cocktail shaker with ice. Add the tequila, lime juice, vinegar, and agave syrup to the cocktail shaker and shake vigorously. Strain into the tumbler. Garnish with the lime wedge and serve.

SERVES 1

Pink peppercorn salt (page 164) or kosher salt, for coating glass rim

Ice

2 ounces 100 percent agave blanco or reposado tequila

1 1/2 ounces freshly squeezed lime juice

1/4 ounce chile vinegar (page 165)

1 ounce agave syrup (page 163)

1 lime wedge

Paloma

Pink peppercorn salt
(page 164) for coating
glass rim

Ice

1³/₄ ounces 100 percent
agave tequila,
preferably blanco

³/₄ ounce St-Germain
liqueur

1 ounce freshly squeezed
grapefruit juice

¹/₂ ounce freshly squeezed
lime juice

¹/₂ ounce Jarritos
grapefruit soda

¹/₂ grapefruit wheel

This classic Mexican cocktail might be Joe's favorite drink of all time. Jarritos is the soda brand traditionally used, but if you can't find it at your local market, substitute Sprite or even Squirt. You can also use kosher salt for coating the rim. We add a bit of floral St-Germain, an elderflower liqueur that really takes it up a notch. You might even call it elegant.

Coat the rim of a 10-ounce tumbler with the salt (see page 158). Fill the tumbler and a cocktail shaker with ice. Add the tequila, liqueur, grapefruit juice, and lime juice to the cocktail shaker and shake vigorously. Strain into the tumbler and float the grapefruit soda on top. Slide the grapefruit wheel halfway down the side of the glass to garnish, then serve.

Pasión

Kosher salt, for coating
glass rim

Ice

1¹/₂ ounces habanero-
infused tequila (page 169)

1 ounce freshly squeezed
orange juice

1 ounce freshly squeezed
lime juice

1 ounce agave syrup
(page 163)

¹/₂ ounce passion fruit puree

1 lime wedge

People who love the place where heat meets sweet can't get enough of this aptly named cocktail with its spicy, tropical rush (although someone we know calls it the Deep Throat, because of the way the chile-laced tequila makes its way down). For the passion fruit puree, we recommend the passion fruit concentrate produced by The Perfect Purée of Napa Valley (perfectpuree.com). Of course, if you're so lucky to have access to fresh passion fruit juice—a true treat in the United States—by all means use it! Just add more agave syrup to taste. *Pictured on page 160.*

Coat the rim of a 10-ounce tumbler with the salt (see page 158). Fill the tumbler and a cocktail shaker with ice. Add the tequila, orange juice, lime juice, agave syrup, and passion fruit puree to the cocktail shaker and shake vigorously. Strain into the tumbler. Garnish with the lime wedge and serve.

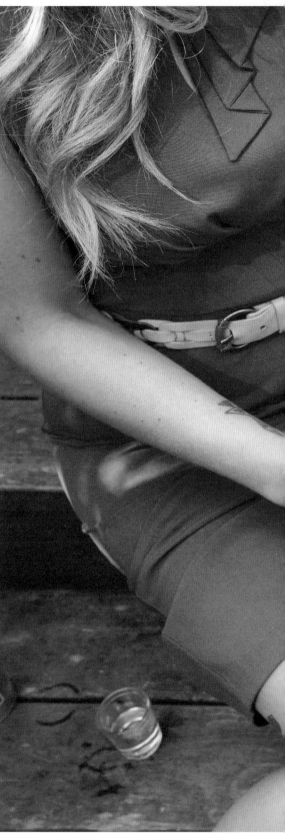

Lolita squeeze

SERVES 1

Chile salt (page 164), for coating glass rim and flavoring

Ice

4 or 5 sprigs cilantro

2 ounces watermelon juice (see note)

2 ounces 100 percent agave tequila, preferably blanco

1 ounce freshly squeezed lime juice

$^1/_2$ ounce agave syrup (page 163)

Fresh watermelon juice is given the tequila treatment here for the ultimate refreshing summer cocktail. The juice is easy to make but doesn't keep well, so make only as much as you can use within a day or so. The chile salt gives it a bit of a wake-up call, but you could skip it if you want something purely pretty in pink.

Coat the rim of a 10-ounce tumbler with the salt (see page 158), then fill the tumbler with ice. Put 3 or 4 of the cilantro sprigs and a pinch of the salt in a cocktail shaker and muddle together with a muddler or a wooden spoon. Fill the shaker with ice, add the watermelon juice, tequila, lime juice, and agave syrup and shake vigorously. Strain into the tumbler. Garnish with the remaining cilantro sprig and serve.

Fresh watermelon juice

To make the watermelon juice, scoop flesh from a ripe seedless watermelon, puree it in a blender until liquefied, and strain it through a fine-mesh sieve. Store in an airtight container in the refrigerator for no more than a day or two.

Mucho gusto

SERVES 1

Toasted-coconut salt
(page 164), for coating
glass rim

Ice

1¹/₂ ounces pineapple-
infused tequila (page 169)

1 ounce coconut water

1 ounce freshly squeezed
lime juice

1 ounce agave syrup
(page 163)

1 lime wedge

Coconut water might be the tastiest health trend to hit the market in the past few years. So why not sully its goody-two-shoes reputation and mix it with some tequila? Great idea, we thought. The result has the classic flavor profile as a piña colada (if slightly lighter), so try rum as a nice alternative to tequila.

Coat the rim of a 10-ounce tumbler with the salt (see page 158). Fill the tumbler and a cocktail shaker with ice. Add the tequila, coconut water, lime juice, and agave syrup to the cocktail shaker and shake vigorously. Strain into the tumbler. Garnish with the lime wedge and serve.

If Honey could drink

SERVES 1

Kosher salt, for coating
glass rim

Ice

1¹/₂ ounces 100 percent
agave tequila

1 ounce cucumber juice
(page 166)

1 ounce freshly squeezed
lime juice

1 ounce agave syrup
(page 163)

1 cucumber wheel

This cocktail is named after our late mild-mannered dog, may she rest in peace. Although her name was Honey, this cucumber-based drink actually has a refreshing and balanced (see: "mild mannered") quality to it reminiscent of a spa beverage—that is, if spas had bars, which would be something we could get with.

Coat the rim of a 10-ounce tumbler with the salt (see page 158). Fill the tumbler and a cocktail shaker with ice. Add the tequila, cucumber juice, lime juice, and agave syrup to the cocktail shaker and shake vigorously. Strain into the tumbler. Garnish with the cucumber wheel and serve.

La siesta

Fresh tarragon, with its hint of anise flavor, is one of the more bewitching fresh herbs around and, outside of the French canon, one of the most underutilized. That's exactly why we turn to it occasionally at Tacolicious, even at the bar. The base of blood orange juice makes a particularly gorgeous cocktail.

Coat the rim of a Collins glass with the salt (see page 158), then fill the glass with ice. Put the sprig of tarragon in a cocktail shaker and muddle with a muddler or a wooden spoon. Fill the cocktail shaker with ice, add the tequila, blood orange juice, lime juice, and agave syrup, and shake vigorously. Strain into the glass and float the soda water on top. Garnish with the blood orange wheel and serve.

SERVES 1

Kosher salt, for coating glass rim

Ice

1 sprig tarragon

2 ounces 100 percent agave tequila, preferably blanco

1 ounce freshly squeezed blood orange juice

1 ounce freshly squeezed lime juice

1 ounce agave syrup (page 163)

Splash of soda water

1 blood orange wheel

Mexican traitor

Although we typically favor cocktails made with tequila, we have a weakness for this rum-based concoction. With a touch of heat from Fresno chiles, it has a sophisticated but beachy element to it that would be right at home at a sophisticated Mexican seaside resort. For the rum, our preference is Brugal. This is one of the few cocktail recipes in this book served straight up (sans ice).

Put 3 of the chile slices in a cocktail shaker and muddle with a muddler or wooden spoon. Fill the shaker with ice, add the rum, pineapple juice, lime juice, and agave syrup, and shake vigorously. Strain straight up into a martini glass. Float the remaining chile slice on top to garnish, then serve.

SERVES 1

4 Fresno chile slices

Ice

1 1/2 ounces dark rum

1 ounce unsweetened pineapple juice

1/2 ounce freshly squeezed lime juice

1/2 ounce agave syrup (page 163)

Flor de Jamaica

There are many riffs on the margarita, but this is one of our favorites. The tea made with *flor de jamaica* (aka hibiscus flowers) lends a puckery, tart quality and a beautiful pink color. It's the ideal summery drink.

Coat the rim of a 10-ounce tumbler with the salt (see page 158). Fill the tumbler and a cocktail shaker with ice. Add the tequila, agave syrup, lime juice, lemon juice, and tea to the cocktail shaker and shake vigorously. Strain into the tumbler. Garnish with the lemon wedge and serve.

Kosher salt, for coating glass rim

Ice

2 ounces 100 percent agave tequila

1 ounce agave syrup (page 163)

$^1/_2$ ounce freshly squeezed lime juice

$^1/_2$ ounce freshly squeeze lemon juice

$^1/_2$ ounce hibiscus tea (page 166)

1 lemon wedge

El sangre

This is a great cocktail to break out in the winter months when tart-sweet blood oranges are in season. You could use regular oranges as a substitute, tasting to adjust for their additional sweetness. The addition of cinnamon is a little ode to holiday spirit, and the smoky mezcal brings to mind a fireplace.

Coat the rim of a 10-ounce tumbler with the salt (see page 158). Fill the tumbler and a cocktail shaker with ice. Add the mezcal, orange juice, agave syrup, and lime juice to the cocktail shaker and shake vigorously. Strain into the tumbler. Garnish with the lime wedge and serve.

Chile salt (page 164), for coating glass rim

Ice

2 ounces mezcal, such as Del Maguey Vida

1 ounce freshly squeezed blood orange juice

1 ounce cinnamon-and-spice agave syrup (page 163)

$^1/_2$ ounce freshly squeezed lime juice

1 lime wedge

Michelada

SERVES 1

Kosher salt, for coating glass rim

Ice

1 (12-ounce) can Tecate or other light Mexican beer

$1/2$ ounce freshly squeezed lime juice

4 dashes of Tapatío or other hot sauce

2 dashes of Maggi sauce

Mexican beer is great, but Mexican beer with lime juice, hot sauce, and a couple shakes of Maggi is better. Yes, Maggi, a condiment typically found in Mexican markets, has MSG in it, but it adds a great savory quality to this classic cocktail. (And hey, life is short.) If you are still not convinced, use a little Worcestershire sauce in its place.

Coat the rim of a pint glass with the salt (see page 158), then fill the glass with ice. Pour in the beer, add the lime juice, hot sauce, and Maggi sauce, stir gently to mix, and serve.

Bucanero

SERVES 1

Ice

2 ounces unsweetened pineapple juice

$1 1/2$ ounces spiced rum such as Kraken

1 ounce freshly squeezed lime juice

1 ounce agave syrup (page 163)

$1/2$ ounce pink guava puree

$1/4$ ounce allspice dram

1 pineapple wedge

Here, just as we do for our Pasión cocktail on page 172, we turn to The Perfect Purée of Napa Valley for the best tropical fruit concentrate, this time the pink guava. Kerns makes a fine, if sweeter, alternative. Allspice dram (also known as pimento dram) is a boldly flavored liqueur that originated in Jamaica, which makes it a natural addition to this rum-based cocktail. Only a touch is needed for great effect.

Fill a 10-ounce tumbler and a cocktail shaker with ice. Add the pineapple juice, rum, lime juice, agave syrup, pink guava puree, and liqueur to the cocktail shaker and shake vigorously. Strain into the tumbler. Garnish with the pineapple wedge and serve.

Sangrita

In Mexico, this tomato-based drink is tequila's BFF. Reminiscent of a sweet Bloody Mary base, *sangrita* is meant to be sipped alternately with a good tequila. (Repeat until the tequila is gone. And then repeat again. You'll get the hang of it quickly.) Our *sangrita* takes a few liberties in the gourmet department by using a tomato sauce made with oven-roasted chiles and garlic and leaving the sweet onion (and do make sure it's a *sweet* onion like Walla Walla or Vidalia) raw for a little bite. The effort is worth the payoff, not to mention that it leaves you with enough *sangrita* to give you an excuse to drink tequila for a good week.

Preheat the oven to 350°F.

Place the chiles, tomatoes, and garlic in a single layer in a small baking pan or dish and cover with aluminum foil. Place in the oven for about 1 hour, until cooked through and soft. Transfer to a bowl and let cool.

Add the onion and cilantro to the cooled vegetables and stir to mix. Then, using a potato masher, mash everything together. Transfer the mashed mixture to a fine-mesh sieve placed over a bowl. Using the back of a wooden spoon, push the mixture through the sieve into the bowl.

Add the grapefruit juice and orange juice and mix well. Season to taste with salt. Transfer to an airtight container and refrigerate until well chilled before serving. It will keep for up to 5 days, though the flavor will get stronger with time.

The ultimate triumverate

At Tacolicious, we have a popular prix fixe menu: a shot of tequila *blanco*, a cold can of Tecate, and a taco for ten dollars. It's what we might call the Holy Trinity, if it weren't a bit blasphemous. Lucky for your friends, you now have the option with this book of serving this ultimate triumvirate to them gratis. We promise that they will be very worshipful.

MAKES ABOUT 2¹/₂ CUPS

1¹/₂ jalapeño chiles, stemmed and halved lengthwise

5 Roma tomatoes, halved lengthwise

2 cloves garlic, lightly crushed

¹/₄ cup finely chopped sweet onion

¹/₄ cup loosely packed chopped fresh cilantro

³/₄ cup freshly squeezed grapefruit juice

³/₄ cup freshly squeezed orange juice

Kosher salt

Sangrita (left) and its friend tequila (right)

Bloody Maria

A Bloody Mary is one thing for brunch. A Bloody Maria is another. Our version takes the punch of tequila and meets it square on with a homemade roasted tomato sauce enlivened with ginger, horseradish, and garlic. Garnished with our *escabache*, it provides a serious wake-up call.

Mix

4 cups diced tomatoes

5 cloves garlic, crushed

¹/₂ cup chopped yellow onion

2 Fresno chiles, stemmed, halved lengthwise, and seeded

¹/₂ cup diced celery

¹/₄ cup soy sauce

¹/₄ cup freshly squeezed lime juice

1 tablespoon finely chopped, peeled fresh ginger

1 tablespoon prepared horseradish

¹/₂ teaspoon celery salt

¹/₂ teaspoon freshly ground black pepper

Kosher salt, for coating glass rims

Ice

8 ounces 100 percent agave tequila, preferably blanco

Pickled cauliflower, carrots, and jalapeños (page 42), optional

4 lime wedges

Preheat the oven to 400°F.

To make the mix, spread 3 cups of the tomatoes, plus the garlic, onion, and chiles on a rimmed baking sheet and roast for 35 minutes, until softened and a bit charred. Remove from the oven and let cool.

In a blender, combine the cooled roasted vegetables, the remaining 1 cup diced tomatoes, and the celery and puree on high speed until smooth. Pass the puree through a fine-mesh sieve placed over a bowl, forcing through as much liquid as possible with the back of a wooden spoon.

Add the soy sauce, lime juice, ginger, horseradish, celery salt, and pepper and mix well. You should have about 2 cups. Chill in the refrigerator.

To assemble each cocktail, coat the rim of a pint glass with the salt (see page 158), then fill the glass with ice. Add ¹/₂ cup (4 ounces) of the mix and 2 ounces of the tequila and stir to mix. Garnish with a spoonful of the pickled vegetables and a lime wedge and serve. Repeat with the remaining 3 cocktails.

Tequila: the CliffsNotes

Soaked in Mexican history and lore, tequila is a subject matter that can be deliberated by spirit geeks until the bartender shouts, "Last call!" But this isn't a book about tequila. This is about drinking for the fun of it, so we'll leave the tome of information for next time. For now, all you need are some smart talking points to get you through the dinner party.

Tequila isn't made from a cactus. In fact, it's made from blue agave, a beautiful, dusty blue-green succulent that resembles a giant aloe plant. In the tequila regions of Mexico, you'll see spiky rows of agave everywhere, just like you see grapes being grown in the wine regions of the world.

The piña is at the heart of it all. The source of tequila is the *piña*, the pineapple-looking heart of the agave plant that grows underground and takes six to twelve years to reach maturity. It can weigh up to two hundred pounds, which is why a *jimador*, the agave farmer who harvests the *piña* with a lethally sharp tool called a *coa*, is such a stud. To make tequila traditionally, the *piña* is first cooked in a stone-walled oven until the flesh is reduced to a soft mass and tastes somewhat like a baked sweet potato (take a whiff of tequila and you can sometimes detect this yammy aroma). Next, the flesh is crushed or milled and the extracted juices are allowed to ferment. The fermented juices are then distilled and sometimes barrel aged.

The mixto is worth nixing. The stuff you're going to want to avoid as you develop into a tequila snob is *mixto* tequila, often labeled as "gold." Mexican law requires that tequila must be at least 51 percent agave.

But any tequila that isn't 100 percent blue agave without anything added such as corn liquor, sugar liquor, sugar, and caramel coloring is labeled *mixto* tequila. And yes, this includes the Jose Cuervo Especial you did body shots with in college.

The top-shelf stuff is all agave. The best tequila will always be labeled "100 percent blue agave." One reason to search this out is to be a true connoisseur. Another reason is because it gives you less of a hangover. Within this category, you'll find four choices: *blanco*, *reposado*, *añejo*, and extra *añejo* (see pages 190–91).

Yes, there is tequila terroir. Almost all tequila is produced in the state of Jalisco, the capital of which is the beautiful city of Guadalajara. There are two regions within this area, the lowlands (aka The Valley of Tequila) and the highlands (aka Los Altos). The lowlands produce a deep, rich, and herbaceous tequila, and the highlands tend to turn out something much fruitier and spicier.

Sipping is better than shooting. In Mexico, and among tequila cognescenti everywhere, good tequila is enjoyed neat and generally sipped, just as you would any quality spirit. The whole lick of salt and big suck of lime ritual should be left to spring breakers. Tequila is also traditionally served with a small glass of *sangrita* (for our recipe, turn to page 185).

Raw fish is it's friend. Although we're not proponents of pairing cocktails or spirits with particular dishes, we do think tequila goes especially well with raw fish dishes, particularly those with a hint of chile. Think ceviches and *aguachiles*.

Falling in love with 7 Leguas

As the saying (kind of) goes, a drink in need is a friend indeed. But when you have the privilege of getting to know the person behind the tequila, your relationship with a spirit grows even deeper.

Such is the case with the excellent 7 Leguas, a small, family-owned distillery in the gorgeous, hilly town of Atotonilco, in the highlands of tequila country. Over the years, members of the Tacolicious staff have often traveled to 7 Leguas. For example, Paul Madonna, our "resident" restaurant artist, flew down to Atotonilco to drink tequila and sketch the village for our massive Palo Alto–location mural. And then there was the time Mike Barrow went to visit.

Mike, the healthiest beverage director in the history of restaurants, hadn't eaten meat for eleven years—until he spent time at 7 Leguas. But before you judge, know that his one moment of pork weakness came out of respect—respect for the 7 Leguas family who not only gave him a tour of the well-cared-for distillery and let him try his hand in the agave fields but also invited him into their *hacienda* for lunch and then, for dinner, took him to their ranch house, which sits in the middle of agave fields, looking toward the mountains. The agave plants glowed in the light of the full moon.

"We were with them for eight hours, talking and hanging out," says Mike. "The owner, Juan Fernando, didn't say much at first. But when he got a little buzz on, he started speaking in English and he was really funny—a great guy. You can tell his family comes first. They're just really cool people." Throughout the dinner, they sipped tequila (Mike is now a huge fan of 7 Leguas *blanco*) and ate pescaterian-friendly dishes like shrimp ceviche. "They love the name Tacolicious. Whenever the cooks placed any food on the table," Mike said, "they'd say, *Tortillalicious!* and all laugh."

But when it came to the last course, the cooks served pork. Mike hesitated only a moment. And then dug in. The verdict? "It was amazing!" he said. "I fell in love with that family. How could I say no?"

Styles of tequilla

Blanco

Easy to identify because it is almost always clear, blanco (white, aka silver or plata) tequila is stored in stainless-steel tanks for no more than sixty days. This style gives the drinker a great chance to taste the origin of the tequila, and the style of the producer.

Reposado

This is "rested" tequila—or kicked back, as we like to think of it. It has been aged in virgin oak for at least two months but for no more than one year, which results in a mellower vibe than a blanco tequila but not as distinctly oak flavored as an añejo. Because it delivers a happy medium, it tends to be our everyday go-to tequila for sipping (though we like them all).

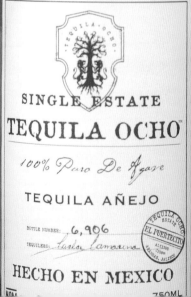

SINGLE ESTATE

TEQUILA OCHO™

100% Puro De Agave

TEQUILA AÑEJO

BOTTLE NUMBER: 6,906

TEQUILERO:

HECHO EN MEXICO

750ML

EST. 1952

Añejo

This tequila has been "aged" in oak for a minimum of one year. It is smooth, complex, rich, and often pricey, which means that we don't recommend it for cocktails. This is what you pour when you want to relax into a glass of tequila. It's great for drinking in the winter, preferably fireside.

Extra añejo

This is the newest category of the four, and it applies to tequilas that are aged in a barrel for a minimum of three years. If you're a bourbon drinker, this one's for you.

40% Alc. Vol.   NET.CONT. 750ml

TEQUILA

FORTALEZA™

Aguas frescas and other G-rated drinks

In the States, Mexican food definitely has a reputation for going down best with booze, but I'd argue that the country celebrates healthy, fresh juices as much as anywhere else. Mexicans have long had a deep appreciation for the freshly squeezed. The most humble street stands serve up made-to-order orange juice and carrot juice, and entire stores specialize in *aguas frescas* (a mix of fruit, citrus, and sugar) and *licuados* (a mix of fruit, milk, and ice).

At Tacolicious, we serve gallons of *aguas frescas* to both kids and adults. We keep them true to the seasons, using only the ripest fresh fruit. These recipes are just the beginning of the numerous things you can do. Experiment with mixing and matching different fruits. Try adding a bit of chile for a spike of heat or a little fresh ginger for a spicy, peppery accent. You can also use different herbs, such as basil or mint. Even cilantro will work if you pair it with something sweet and acidic like pineapple.

Cantaloupe-ginger agua fresca

Fresh ginger gives the mild, sweet cantaloupe a good punch. Any ripe melon, such as honeydew, Charentais, or even watermelon (taking into consideration watermelon will offer a lot more juice), can be substituted for the cantaloupe.

In a blender, combine the ginger and 1/2 cup of the water and puree for about 30 seconds until somewhat smooth. Strain through a fine-mesh sieve into a pitcher.

Rinse out the blender canister, then return it to its base. Combine the cantaloupe, sugar, lemon juice, and 1/2 cup water in the blender and puree on high speed until very smooth. Add to the pitcher holding the ginger water, then stir in the remaining 6 cups water. Serve in tall glasses over ice.

MAKES ABOUT 8 CUPS;
SERVES 6

1/2-inch piece fresh ginger, peeled

7 cups cold water

3 cups deseeded, coarsely chopped cantaloupe

1 cup sugar

1 teaspoon freshly squeezed lemon juice

Ice

Cucumber-mint agua fresca

Cucumber juice, with the addition of sugar and lemon juice, is the perfect beverage for sipping on a hot summer day.

In a blender, combine the cucumber, sugar, mint leaves, and lemon juice and puree on high speed for about 30 seconds, until smooth. Strain through a fine-mesh sieve into a pitcher. Stir in the water. Serve in tall glasses over ice and garnish with the mint sprigs.

MAKES ABOUT 8 CUPS;
SERVES 6

3 cups coarsely chopped unpeeled English cucumber

1 cup sugar

1/4 cup packed fresh mint leaves, plus sprigs, for garnish

3 1/2 tablespoons freshly squeezed lemon juice

6 1/2 cups cold water

Ice

Mango agua fresca

MAKES ABOUT 8 CUPS;
SERVES 6

2 1/4 cups peeled, coarsely chopped mangoes

1 cup sugar

3 tablespoons freshly squeezed lemon juice

6 cups cold water

Ice

This is tropical paradise in a cup. If you can find Kent mangoes—the delicious green-skinned specimens with meaty, juicy, ambrosia-like flesh—you've hit gold. Manila mangoes, which are a bit tarter, are a good second choice.

In a blender, combine the mangoes, sugar, lemon juice, and 1 cup of the water and puree on high speed for about a minute or until smooth. Pour into a pitcher and stir in the remaining 5 cups water adding a bit more if necessary. Serve in tall glasses over ice.

Pineapple-coconut agua fresca

MAKES ABOUT 8 CUPS;
SERVES 6

2 cups coarsely chopped fresh pineapple

3/4 cup sugar

3/4 cup unsweetened pineapple juice

1/3 cup coconut milk

2 tablespoons freshly squeezed lemon juice

5 cups cold water

Ice

The classic combo that makes a piña colada so delicious also works without the booze.

In a blender, combine the pineapple, sugar, pineapple juice, coconut milk, and lemon juice and puree on high speed for about 1 minute, until smooth. Strain through a fine-mesh sieve into a pitcher. Stir in the water. Serve in tall glasses over ice.

Kiwi agua fresca

MAKES ABOUT 8 CUPS;
SERVES 6

5 kiwi, peeled, the small
pit at the top removed, and
coarsely chopped

3/4 cup sugar

1/3 cup freshly squeezed
lemon juice

7 cups cold water

Ice

There's something about the combination of the vivid green flesh and the crunchy black seeds of kiwifruits that makes this drink seem exotic. It's a perfect refreshment for the colder months when you're lamenting the loss of summer produce.

In a blender, combine the kiwifruits, sugar, and lemon juice and puree on high speed for about 1 minute, until smooth. Pour into a pitcher and stir in the water. Taste and adjust the sweetness and acidity as needed. Serve in tall glasses over ice.

White nectarine–blueberry agua fresca

MAKES ABOUT 8 CUPS;
SERVES 6

1 cup fresh blueberries

4 1/2 cups cold water

4 white nectarines, pitted
and coarsely chopped

1 cup sugar

3 1/2 tablespoons freshly
squeezed lemon juice

Ice

You can smell the perfume of perfectly ripe white nectarines from across the room. Pair the nectarines with the best crisp-tart blueberries you can find (not the mushy, bland ones that are blueberry imposters) to make this inspired *agua fresca*. Peeled and pitted white peaches can be substituted for the nectarines.

In a small saucepan, combine the blueberries and 1/2 cup of the water over medium-low heat and bring to a simmer. Cook for about 5 minutes, until the berries just start to break down a bit. Transfer the berry mixture to a blender and puree for a few seconds. Strain through a fine-mesh sieve into a pitcher.

Rinse out the blender canister and return it to its base. Add the nectarines, sugar, and lemon juice to the blender and puree on high speed for about 1 minute, until smooth. Strain through a fine-mesh sieve into the pitcher with the blueberry juice. Stir in the remaining 4 cups water. Serve in tall glasses over ice.

Homemade horchata

Not all beverages under the *aguas frescas* umbrella have fruit in them. This classic rice-based refresher, which was introduced to Mexico by the Spanish, is laced with cinnamon and vanilla and is like drinking a milky, icy pudding. Other variations on *horchata* can be found in Mexico, including ones that include almonds and fruit. In our opinion, most taquerias that we know make their *horchata* wincingly sweet. So, although this recipe is far from sugar free, it will please kids without knocking the adults off their feet. If you want to be a little fancy, garnish each drink with a cinnamon stick.

In a bowl, combine the rice, cinnamon stick, vanilla bean, and 4 cups of the water, cover, and refrigerate for at least 4 hours or overnight.

Transfer the rice mixture to a blender and puree on high speed for 2 to 3 minutes, until as smooth as possible. Strain through a chinois or through a fine-mesh sieve lined with cheesecloth into a bowl, using the back of a wooden spoon to help push it all through. (If you are using a sieve and don't have cheesecloth, strain the mixture twice.) Discard the solids.

Rinse out the blender canister and return it to its base. Pour the rice liquid back into the blender. Add the condensed milk, lime juice, vanilla extract, sugar, cinnamon, and salt and puree for about 1 minute, until smooth. Pour into a pitcher and stir in the remaining 3 to 4 cups water, according to taste.

Cover and refrigerate until well chilled before serving. Serve in tall glasses over ice. Top with a light dusting of cinnamon.

MAKES ABOUT 8 CUPS; SERVES 6

2 cups long-grain white rice

1 (2-inch) cinnamon stick, preferably canela (Mexican cinnamon)

$1/4$ vanilla bean

7 to 8 cups water

$1/2$ cup sweetened condensed milk

$1^1/_2$ teaspoons freshly squeezed lime juice

$1/2$ teaspoon vanilla extract

$1/2$ cup sugar

$1/8$ teaspoon ground cinnamon, plus more for garnish

$1/2$ teaspoon kosher salt

Ice

Mia

SERVES 1

Ice

4 ounces freshly squeezed
orange juice

4 ounces cranberry juice

1 ounce freshly squeezed
lime juice

1 ounce agave syrup
(page 163)

2 tablespoons apple-
ginger cocktail salsa
(page 166)

Named after Joe's daughter, Mia, this mocktail is full of life—rocking, even (after all, Mia is excellent on the electric guitar). It's topped with a fruit salsa mixed with a little chile for a mild sneak attack. You could consider the salsa optional, but the drink is not even half as exciting without it. If a crowd is headed over to your place, you can easily whip up a pitcher (see page 150).

Fill a Collins glass and a cocktail shaker with ice. Add the orange juice, cranberry juice, lime juice, and agave syrup to the cocktail shaker and shake vigorously. Strain into the glass. Top with the salsa and serve.

Silas

SERVES 1

8 fresh mint leaves

Ice

2 ounces freshly squeezed
lime juice

1 ounce agave syrup
(page 163)

6 ounces soda water

1 lime wheel

My oldest son, Silas, might have plenty of pop and pep, but he prefers his namesake drink sans bubbles, which is why he orders this *mojito*-inspired mocktail without the fizzy water, *please* (such manners!). If you prefer his way, just replace the soda water with still water.

Put the mint leaves in a pint glass and muddle them with a muddler or wooden spoon. Fill the glass with ice, add the lime juice, agave syrup, and soda water, and stir well. Garnish with the lime wheel and serve.

Silas, Moss, and Mia with their respective drinks.

Moss

The youngest of the three siblings, my son Moss used to be called out as the "juice-aholic" in the family. Although he has largely kicked the habit, he still dabbles. We turn to The Perfect Purée of Napa Valley (perfectpuree.com), which makes an excellent passion fruit concentrate. If you can't find it, just look for a quality brand that's not full of sugar.

Fill a pint glass and a cocktail shaker with ice. Add the pineapple juice, lime juice, and passion fruit puree to the cocktail shaker and shake vigorously. Strain into the glass, add the soda water, and stir well. Garnish with the pineapple wedge and serve.

SERVES 1

Ice

2 ounces unsweetened pineapple juice

1 ounce freshly squeezed lime juice

1 ounce passion fruit puree or passion fruit juice

6 ounces soda water

1 pineapple wedge

Ingredients glossary

Achiote paste

In Mexico, markets sell piles of different types of *recados*, or "pastes." This traditional one is a deep red from annatto seeds and made with varying ingredients, such as sour orange; spices such as allspice, cloves, and coriander; garlic; and salt. It's frequently used in the Yucatán, where it flavors everything from seafood to pork (we use it in our version of *cochinita pibil* on page 126). Although you can make it yourself, it's also available at most Mexican markets. We like the El Mexicano brand.

Avocados

Avocados vary a lot in size and meatiness, which is why our recipes often call for a measured amount rather than a specific number of fruits. Although roughly one thousand avocado varieties exist, you'll only see a handful of them in U.S. markets, among them the Pinkerton, Reed, Bacon, Gillogly, and Gwen. The Hass avocado, however, makes up 90 percent of U.S. sales. Luckily, as avocados go, it's a good one, with its buttery taste and texture. Look for avocados at Latin markets, where they tend to cost about half as much as they do at regular supermarkets.

Banana leaves

Banana leaves are used for wrapping food before it goes onto the grill or into the oven and for making tamales. They impart a fragrance that's a bit herbal—not surprisingly, it's reminiscent of a green banana. If you happen to have a banana tree in your yard, forage away (just rinse the leaves well and remove the center vein before using). But if you're like most of us, you'll find banana leaves in plastic bags in the freezer section of Latin and Asian markets. To thaw a banana leaf, leave it out at room temperature until soft and pliable.

Cheeses

We can blame old-school Mexican-American restaurants with their cheese-laden combo plates for making people think that Mexican food is unhealthy. But the truth is, cheese doesn't play a leading role in the cuisine, and when it does appear, it commonly acts as a delicious accent. For the best selection of Mexican cheeses, go to a Latin market, where the cheeses are usually displayed in a refrigerated section or behind the counter. If that's not possible, many supermarkets carry a range of Mexican cheeses packaged by brands such as El Mexicano.

Cotija (queso añejo) This aged cheese, usually made from cow's milk, has a salty, crumbly quality that makes it good for tossing in salads. It's also the cheese used on the classic Mexican street food treat of corn on the cob.

Oaxaca This soft, stretched cow's milk curd cheese is wound into balls. It can be cooked directly on the griddle, but it's also good in quesadillas or anything in which you want a stretchy, melty cheese.

Queso fresco At Tacolicious, we make our own *queso fresco* from cow's milk. The result is mild, fresh, and falls somewhere between ricotta in its sweetness and a creamy feta in its texture. We use it in all sorts of things, including the mix for our meatballs (page 80). However, very good *queso fresco* can be found at Latin markets, sold prepacked or fresh by the pound.

Chicharrónes

Blistered and crispy, fresh (not packaged) *chicharrónes* are usually found in Latin markets under a heat lamp to keep them warm. In Mexico, they are eaten, often seasoned with chile and lime, as a crisp snack like chips, but they are also softened in a salsa to make tacos or to make one killer *torta*.

Chiles

Fresh and dried chiles are one of the biggest anchors of Mexican cuisine and within this culinary tradition there are endless varieties to choose from (especially dried). However, the following chiles are the ones that we use at the restaurant the most. They're also ones that you should be able to find relatively easily at not just Mexican markets, but American ones, too.

Fresh chiles

Fresno This chile, generally sold red, looks like a jalapeño, with a sharper tip. It tends to be medium in its heat level and has a sweet flavor.

Habanero According to the Scoville scale, which measures the spicy heat of chiles, this small, orange, floral bell-shaped chile used throughout the Yucatán is one of the hottest. We call for it in a number of recipes, but we make sure to temper its heat with other additions to ensure the dish isn't too fiery to enjoy.

Jalapeño The jalapeño is almost always sold green instead of the red it turns when it ripens. Of all the fresh chiles, it varies the most in heat level from pepper to pepper, which means you'll need to rely on your taste buds to guide you. Also, the jalapeños grown today—like so much produce, sadly—are often gargantuan. This is why, when chopped jalapeños are used in a recipe, we call for a measured amount rather than a number of whole chiles.

Poblano In the United States, you'll often find this glossy, dark green chile mislabeled as a pasilla chile. (A true pasilla negro is a dried version of a chilaca chile.) Grassy and vegetative in flavor, poblanos are almost always roasted and peeled before they are eaten, and even though they are generally pretty mild, their heat level can vary dramatically. A dried poblano is called an ancho chile, another popular chile in the Tacolicious kitchen.

Serrano Slightly hotter than a jalapeño, this long, skinny chile is, like the jalapeño, more commonly sold green than red. If you prefer the flavor and heat of the serrano over the jalapeño, you can substitute it—just use your discretion.

Jalapeño

Fresno

Serrano   Poblano

Habanero

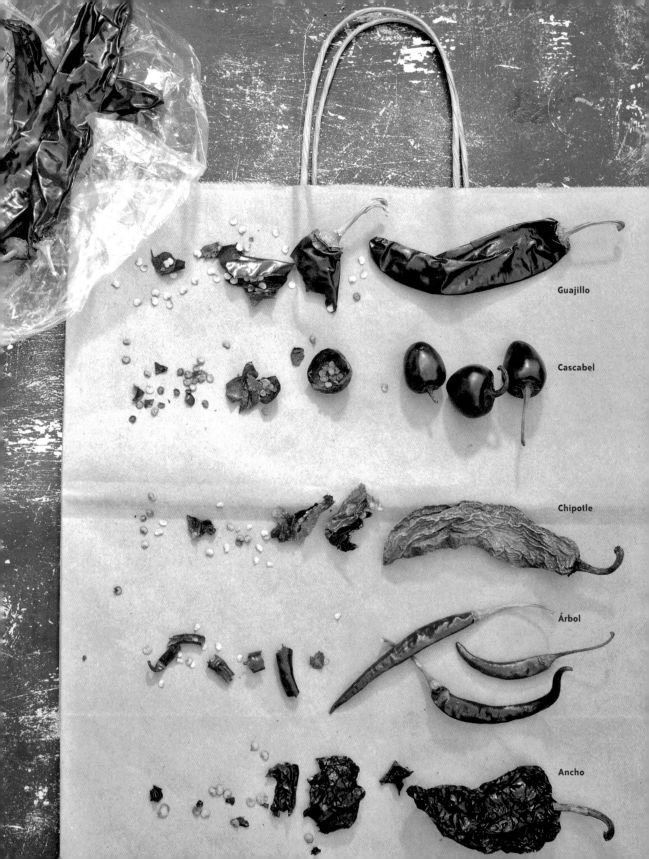

Guajillo

Cascabel

Chipotle

Árbol

Ancho

Dried chiles

Ancho A dried poblano chile, this medium-size, raisin-colored, wrinkled pepper is shaped like an elongated heart. It has a bit of a sweetness to it, which might be why it's so popular.

Árbol Only about 2 inches long, this skinny, pointed chile stays brick red even after drying. Its heat level ranges from medium to searing, so use with caution.

Cascabel These cute little round chiles get their name from the percussive shake-a-shake sound the seeds make. The skin is smooth and the heat level is medium.

Chipotle A smoked and dried jalapeño, the chipotle has become well known in recent years, in large part because a Mexican chain restaurant decided to name itself after the chile. The decision is understandable: the smoky sweetness of the chipotle is addictive. Chipotles are widely sold canned in red adobo sauce (a tomato sauce with a vinegary edge). Dusty brown, ridged dried chipotles are also available.

Guajillo This is one of our favorite chiles. Mild, with a little kick, it's used to flavor all sorts of marinades and sauces, including the one in which we braise our short ribs (page 102).

Cilantro

Life would not be as nice without cilantro. The dried seeds of the plant are known as coriander, a spice that isn't used much in Mexican cooking. But the delicate, almost lacy, fresh green leaves are employed prolifically as an herb. The stems are generally tender enough to chop along with the leaves, but if you want to be fancy, pluck the leaves off before prepping. Just never chop cilantro too vigorously or you risk turning it into a pile of mush. The fragrance of cilantro is a bit soapy—and much different from the hearty, peppery scent of flat-leaf parsley, the only herb you might confuse it with. So if you are not sure whether you have grabbed the correct bunch, give it a sniff before you buy.

Crema

With its nice tang and creamy, almost pourable texture, this is the sour cream or crème fraîche of Mexico (and yes, those two ingredients make acceptable substitutes). Look for it at Latin markets, though some mainstream supermarkets also carry it. If you want to try your hand at making our version, turn to page 37.

Cumin

One of the most ubiquitous spices in Mexican cooking, cumin seeds have an aroma that's slightly earthy and quite addictive. We'd use it in everything if we could. Although you can buy ground cumin, for the freshest flavor, we highly recommend toasting the seeds and grinding them. To do this, place the seeds in a dry heavy skillet over medium heat and toast until they become fragrant, about 15 to 30 seconds. Transfer to a clean spice grinder, allow to cool, then grind to a powder.

Kosher salt

Compared with overly fine and overly salty iodized (table) salt, the much flakier kosher salt is easier to grasp between your fingers, allowing for more control. That control is what makes kosher salt a favorite of chefs. The coarser texture also means that our salt measurements are not interchangeable with table salt. In fact, we only recommend Diamond brand kosher salt for this book. Morton's, another popular brand, is inexplicably much saltier.

Mexican oregano

Oregano—particularly dried oregano—is used a lot in Mexican cooking. You can use the sweeter Mediterranean oregano in its place, but because it does not even belong to the same botanical family, it is quite different from Mexican oregano, which is stronger flavored and more citrusy. Look for dried Mexican oregano in Latin markets.

Nopales

Fresh prickly pear cactus paddles, often kindly already stripped of their thorns before sale, can be found at most Latin and Mexican markets. This nutritious vegetable has a texture with a bit of crunch and a flavor that isn't far from that of the bell pepper. After cutting up the paddles, rinse the pieces before you use them, as they can be a bit mucilaginous. When nopales are cooked, they lose their bright green color. We also like them blended raw with pineapple and orange to make a great *agua fresca*.

Tamarind

A little sweet and a lot tart, tamarind comes from a tree that produces big, brown seed-filled pods that conceal the flavorful pulp. Tamarind is sold in pulp form (with the seeds still in it) or the more practical seedless paste form and can be found in markets catering to Southeast Asian, Indian, or Mexican consumers. (You can also buy the whole pods, but it is time-consuming to free the pulp from around the seeds.) Tamarind pastes, which we recommend using, vary in their concentration, so use them judiciously.

Tomatillos

The tomatillo, which is native to Mexico, is harvested green, is covered with a paperlike brown husk, and tastes vaguely like a green tomato. Not surprisingly, tomatillos, which are part of the nightshade family, are used a bit like tomatoes in Mexican cooking, where they are often grilled or used fresh in salsas. They are also the key ingredient in the popular *chile verde* (page 129). Look for tomatillos that are taut and firm, a sign of freshness.

Tortillas

Corn tortillas are the heart of Mexican cuisine and have been since the days of the Aztecs. Corn tortillas are made from dried maize, or corn kernels, which are soaked in limewater (slaked lime) to remove their skins. The kernels are then ground, cooked, and formed into a dough that is pressed into tortillas. For more on corn tortillas, see pages 107–8.

Mail-order sources

Globalization is a good thing for the culinarily curious. Today, with a little help from the internet, you can get most everything you need to cook pretty much any cuisine, no matter where you live. Here are our recommendations for sourcing ingredients for the recipes in this book.

The Chile Guy If you're looking for a chile-specific site, this is place to go. • thechileguy.com

Gourmet Sleuth A great place to pick up frozen banana leaves, tamarind paste, and dried chiles, all in a one-stop shop. • gourmetsleuth.com

Melissa's Produce For fresh fruits and vegetables such as tomatillos, chiles, passion fruit, mangoes (like five different varieties), and banana leaves, you can rely on this longtime purveyor of the exotic. • melissasproduce.com

Mex Grocer This comprehensive site sells pretty much every Mexican pantry item you desire, from dried chiles and Mexican oregano to achiote paste and fresh cheeses. • mexgrocer.com

Mi Pueblo Foods Although this great Mexican supermarket chain doesn't have an online store, it does have many brick-and-mortar locations in California, including in the Bay Area, Central Valley, and Central Coast. They even have their own *tortilleria* that makes tortillas to order. • mipueblofoods.com

Old Town Liquor (aka the Tequila Superstore) Though it also sells other spirits, this is a fantastic source for tequila, mezcal, sotol, and pretty much anything made from agave. • zeetequila.com

Perfect Puree Many of the cocktails that we make call for the high-quality fruit purees and concentrates from this Napa Valley–based company. A longtime secret among restaurant industry folks, these products are actually available to the consumer as well. (Note to buyers: Perfect Puree requires a three jar minimum.) • perfectpuree.com

Rancho Gordo We purchase almost all of our dried beans from this Napa Valley–based company. They also sell some dried chiles, dried herbs, rice, and more—not to mention really cute tee-shirts. • ranchogordo.com

Williams-Sonoma Several of our Tacolicious-brand salsas and braising liquids are now available in-store and online. • williams-sonoma.com

Restaurants we love

On a quest for good Mexican restaurants and food stalls, we've traveled throughout Mexico (and in our own California Bay Area backyard, too). This list is by no means complete *(we'd like to emphasize that part), but here are some of our A-listers.*

CALIFORNIA

Casa Vicky's You can't go wrong with the rotisserie chicken dinner at this family restaurant.
792 E Julian Street, San Jose • casavicky.com

La Costa The shrimp cocktail at this San Jose classic was the inspiration for our own rendition (page 61). Theirs is properly served in a tall Styrofoam cup.
1805 Alum Rock Avenue, San Jose • 408-937-1010

La Victoria Taqueria Home of the famous orange sauce (page 35). Enough said.
140 E San Carlos Street, San Jose • lavicsj.com

La Palma The amazing San Francisco–based company that makes our tortillas also makes delicious food to go, as well as banana leaves and unprepared, wet *masa* that you'll need to make the tamales on page 77.
2884 24th Street, San Francisco • lapalmasf.com

La Taqueria One of the most deservedly popular taquerias in SF, La Taqueria's untraditionally large but addictive tacos are served with corn tortillas fried up on the *plancha* (ask for yours "dorado" to get it really crisp).
2889 Mission Street, San Francisco • 415-285-7117

La Torta Gorda One of our favorite spots in San Francisco for *tortas* (especially the *pierna enchilada*), *huitlacoche* quesadillas, *agua frescas*, and more.
2833 24th Street, San Francisco • latortagorda.net

MEXICO

Contramar This lunch-only Mexican brasserie (for lack of a better word) is one of our favorite restaurants in the world. Get the tuna tostada, chopped soft shell crab, *pulpo a la talla*, and more.
Durango 200, Roma, Mexico City • contramar.com.mx

El Califa This awesome, modern taqueria has multiple locations in DF. Everything is good here, but the *nopal y queso* taco is great.
Altata 22, Condesa, Mexico City • elcalifa.com.mx

El Tizoncito Order a dozen *tacos al pastor* and call it a night.
Tamaulitpas 122, Condesa, Mexico City • eltizoncito.com

Hijo de La Rauxa Sit down to a set-price lunch at this tiny little spot (with an ever changing name) in Condesa run by chef Quim Jardi.
Calle Parras 15, Condesa, Mexico City
• facebook.com/laRauxa

Maximo Bistrot A chicly rustic little restaurant in the up-and-coming Roma neighborhood. The chef Eduardo Garcia comes from the lauded Pujol restaurant in DF. Though the food isn't necessarily Mexican, we loved it.
Tonalá 133, Roma, Mexico City • maximobistrot.com

The Restaurant Our friend chef Donnie Masterton, an old friend of Joe's from his days in San Francisco, has relocated to the gorgeous colonial town of San Miguel de Allende and now cooks decidedly California-style food in Mexico. We can't recommend it enough.
Sollano 16, San Miguel de Allende
• therestaurantsanmiguel.com

El Rincón Chiapaneco At this small open-air eatery in the town of Tulum, we order its perfect *panuchos* as well as huge glasses of *hugo verde* (a mix of pineapple juice and juice made from a green similar to spinach).
Calle Jupiter Sur, opposite the ADO stop, Tulum

Index

Copyright © 2014 by Sara Deseran and Joe Hargrave
Photographs copyright © 2014 by Alex Farnum

Published in the United States by Ten Speed Press, an
imprint of the Crown Publishing Group, a division of
Random House LLC, a Penguin Random House Company,
New York.
www.crownpublishing.com
www.tenspeed.com

Ten Speed Press and the Ten Speed Press colophon
are registered trademarks of Random House LLC

Photo on page 189 appears courtesy of the authors.

Library of Congress Cataloging-in-Publication Data
Deseran, Sara.
    Tacolicious : festive recipes for tacos, snacks, cocktails,
and more / Sara Deseran with Joe Hargrave, Antelmo Faria,
and Mike Barrow.
    pages cm
    1. Mexican American cooking. 2. Snack foods. 3. Tacos.
I. Hargrave, Joe. II. Faria, Antelmo. III. Barrow, Mike
(Restauranteur) IV. Title.
    TX715.2.S69D468 2014
    641.5926872073—dc23
                                                          2013051109

Hardcover ISBN: 978-1-60774-562-4
eBook ISBN: 978-1-60774-563-1

Printed in China

Design by Emma Campion
Food and prop styling by Christine Wolheim

10 9 8 7 6 5 4 3 2

First Edition